WILD swimming
Walks

Dartmoor and South Devon
28 lake, river and beach days out

Sophie Pierce

Matt Newbury

WILD
THINGS
PUBLISHING

Sharrah Pool, River Dart

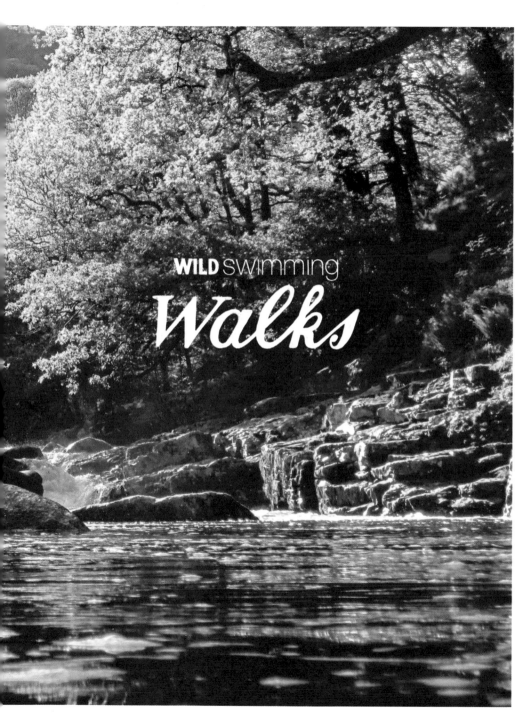

WILD SWIMMING
Walks

Honiton

Whimple

Sidmouth

THE WALKS

No.	NAME	SWIMMING
1	West Okement and Meldon Circular	West Okement River (waterfalls), quarry lake at Meldon Pond
2	East Okement Pools and Taw Marsh Circular	East Okement River (pools and waterfalls), Taw River
3	Shilley Pool Circular	Shilley Pool, Blackaton Brook
4	Teign Gorge Circular	River Teign pools
5	Kestor Rock, Scorhill and Gidleigh Circular	North Teign pools
6	Tavy Cleave Circular	River Tavy pools
7	Sandy Hole and East Dart Waterfall Circular	East Dart pools and waterfall
8	Foggintor Quarry and the Pila Brook Circular	Foggintor Quarry, dipping pools in the Pila Brook
9	The Stepping Stones Walk	West Dart and East Dart pools
10	Crazywell Circular	Crazywell Pool, Hart Tor Waterfall
11	Sharrah Pool Circular	River Dart pools
12	Warhorse Pool and Shavercombe Waterfall Circular	River Plym, Warhorse Pool and Shavercombe Waterfall
13	Central Dartmoor Lakes	Quarry lakes: Leftlake and Red Lake
14	Ivybridge Pools Circular	River Erme pools
15	Mount Batten Peninsular Circular	Sea at Batten Bay and Clovelly Bay. Estuary at Hooe Lake (only at high tide)
16	Cellar Beach Circular	Sea at Cellar Beach, River Yealm estuary at Kilpatrick Steps and other entry points along the river
17	Westcombe and Wonwell Circular	Sea at Westcombe Beach and Wonwell Beach
18	Bantham to Thurlestone Circular	Sea at Bantham Sands, South Milton Sands and Leas Foot Sand. Fun swim through rock arch
19	Soar Mill Cove Circular	Sea at Soar Mill Cove, Starehole Bay, North Sands, South Sands
20	Woodcombe Sands and Ivy Cove Circular	Sea at Woodcombe Cove and Ivy Cove
21	Start Point Circular	Sea at Peartree Point, Great Mattiscombe Sand
22	Beesands to Hallsands Circular	Sea at Hallsands and Beesands
23	Little Dartmouth, Compass Cove, Sugary Cove, Castle Cove Circular	Sea at Compass Cove, Sugary Cove and Castle Cove. Dramatic swim through 'chasm'
24	Mill Bay Circular	Sea at Mill Bay Cove, double cave that can be swum through at high tide
25	Man Sands and Scabbacombe Circular	Sea at Scabbacombe Sands and Man Sands
26	Broadsands to Elberry Cove and Churston Cove Circular	Sea at Broadsands, Elberry Cove, Churston Cove and Fishcombe Cove
27	Staverton Circular	River Dart
28	Teignmouth to Dawlish Railway Walk	Sea at Teignmouth and Dawlish

TERRAIN	REFRESHMENTS EN ROUTE	MILES	DIFFICULTY
Open moor, steep climbs, ancient woodland, marshy areas	None	5	Hard
Open moor, steep climbs, woods. Stone circle	Pub in Belstone (¾ way round)	7	Hard
Moorland village, open moor, steep climbs, country lanes, stone rows	Pubs in South Zeal	4.5	Hard
Woods, climbs, heathland	Café at Castle Drogo (start and finish)	4	Moderate
Open moor, ancient monuments, woods, tors, climbs	None	5	Hard
Open moor, ancient monuments, tors	None	5.5	Hard
Open moor, tors, gradual climbs	Pub and café at Postbridge (start and finish)	5.5	Moderate
Open moor, tors, stone rows, fairly level	None	4	Easy
Open moor, woods, stepping stones, tors, country lanes	Tea room at Dartmeet (¾ way round)	7	Hard
Open moor, rough tracks, stone row, woods, gradual climbs	None	4	Moderate
Woods, open moor, one very steep climb	Pub and café in Holne ⅔ way round)	5	Moderate
Open moor, rough tracks, ancient monuments gradual climbs	None	5	Moderate
Open moor, rough tracks. Fairly level, few big climbs	None	12	Hard (only on account of length)
Woodlands, some climbs, heathland	Pubs and cafes in Ivybridge (start and finish)	3.5	Easy
Low grassy cliffs, coast path through marinas, historic maritime village, naval remains	Pub and café (½ way round)	2.5	Easy
Estuary village, coast path, one gradual climb, woods, cliffs, walk along estuary	Pubs in Noss Mayo (start and finish)	4.5	Easy
Woods, fields, coast path, one very steep climb, cliffs	Pub in Kingston (start and finish)	5	Moderate
Coast path, fields, cliffs, one steep climb	Pubs at Bantham, and Thurlestone (¾ way around). Café at South Milton Sands (half way round),	4	Moderate
Coast path, lanes, fields, some steep climbs, cliffs	Pubs/cafes in Salcombe and Soar Mill Cove Hotel (½ way round)	6	Hard
Coast path, cliffs, fields, some climbs, lanes	Pub and café in East Prawle (start and finish)	5	Easy
Coast path, fields, cliffs, one gradual climb	None	2	Moderate
Coast path, fields, cliffs, sunken lanes, gradual climbs	Pub and seafood shack at Beesands (start and finish)	3	Easy
Coast path, fields, cliffs, woods, gradual climbs	Café at Dartmouth Castle (half way round)	3	Moderate
Coast path, sunken lane, one steep climb other moderate climbs, cliffs	None	3	Moderate
Coast path, fields, some steep climbs	None	2.5	Moderate
Low grassy cliffs, coast path, golf course, woods	Café at Broadsands (start and finish) Pub in Churston (⅔ way round)	3.5	Easy
Fields, riverside walking, fairly flat village lanes	Pub in Staverton (half way round) Café at Staverton Bridge (start and finish)	2	Easy
Coast path along railway line, lanes, main road, some climbs	Cafes and pubs in Teignmouth and Dawlish (start/finish)	3 or 6	Moderate (depending on whether returning by train)

Peartree Point (nr Start Point)

INTRODUCTION

*I*f like us you have a passion for swimming in Britain's wonderful natural playgrounds, you are bound to stumble across uninitiated friends who say things like "Wild swimming? That used to be called just 'swimming' didn't it?" It's a fair point, but the 'wild' bit refers to enjoying the untamed wilderness and getting back to nature in a way that is often missing from 21st century life. It's the chance to go on the sort of adventures that were such an important part of growing up and are now often missing from our busy adult lives. It's a return to the sort of escapades that thrilled us in the pages of our favourite adventure stories, or the kind of exploits that filled our free time when summers lasted forever and escapist play was actively encouraged.

The journey is just as important as the swim itself. While the average person rarely walks more than a few minutes away from their car, unexpected adventures are always waiting around the next corner if you walk even just a few hundred metres more. We want to show you some of Devon's most beautiful routes. Craggy cliffs, serpentine estuaries, bleak moorland, waterfalls, rivers and sparkling seas with coastlines peppered with caves and gullies - South Devon has it all for the walker and swimmer, and we want to infect you with our enthusiasm, as well as share all these breathtaking places.

Every day we think how lucky we are to live here. Devon has such contrasting landscapes, from the red cliffs of Teignmouth, to the limestone buttresses of the South Hams, and the granite tors of Dartmoor. There are so many experiences to share. The community of swimmers that has evolved here in the last few years has been nothing short of extraordinary. Social media has helped us connect with the most enormous variety of people of different ages, sizes and backgrounds, all united by their love of swimming in the great outdoors and exploring the many fascinating places South Devon has to offer.

It all started one freezing cold New Year's Day, quite a few years ago now, before the days of Facebook, when a group of us decided to bring in the New Year with a dip. Clad in ill-fitting surf wetsuits, we ran into the grey sea at Bantham on the South Devon coast, dodging the rollers and plunging in. Afterwards we warmed up with hot toddies around a bonfire, enjoying the camaraderie of facing the elements together. Then we thought – why only do this on high days and holidays? Why not all the time?

And so we met up one evening, round the fire, armed with Ordnance Survey maps, focussing on the bits of blue. We soon had a list of places we wanted to explore, and swims we wanted to do, and we started meeting regularly as a group, and having the most wonderful experiences. We swam down estuaries with the outgoing tide, we explored Dartmoor's waterfalls and pools, and discovered its isolated lakes. We went on swim safaris along the coastline, finding caves and lagoons along the way, and learning a lot about the stunning marine biology of the British coast.

This book is about laughter, old-fashioned adventure, joy and high spirits. It's about exploring one of the most exciting places in the UK, preferably accompanied by lashings of your favourite tipple and quantities of cake. A friend of ours, Jackie, always says "You never regret a swim" and that's so true. Throw in a brisk walk and you are onto a winner. The people we have met also seem to include some of the most talented bakers in the UK, and we've lost count of the amount of delicious home-cooked cake we've enjoyed along the way. Calories definitely don't count if enjoyed as part of a wild swim adventure.

DARTMOOR

"I have wandered over Europe, have rambled to Iceland, climbed the Alps, been for some years lodged among the marshes of Essex – yet nothing I have seen has quenched in me the longing after the fresh air, and love of the wild scenery of Dartmoor."

The Book of Dartmoor by Sabine Baring-Gould

A cursory glance over a map of Dartmoor might suggest that this rugged National Park is somewhat lacking in blue shaded areas. But don't be fooled. Take the time to study the map in more detail (we prefer to do this on winter's evenings by the flickering light of a log fire, while simultaneously quaffing something warming) and the meandering blue scars of rivers and the unnaturally straight lines of man-made leats begin to reveal themselves, as do the life-giving reservoirs and the flooded quarries, the isolated streams and natural pools.

Dartmoor really is a story of water. The Ice Age sculpted the iconic fists of the granite tors, while melting glaciers carved the rivers, leaving boulders carelessly strewn along their twisting routes. It was access to water that brought farmers to the moor from prehistoric times, and water that powered the wheels used in various industries from tin mining to wool production and gun powder manufacture, to an ice factory that supplied the Plymouth fishing industry.

Water has also contributed to the mystery of the moor, with the mists and mires inspiring everyone from Agatha Christie to Arthur Conan Doyle, who set The Hound of the Baskervilles in the wilds of Dartmoor. The isolation and inhospitable landscapes, and myths of marshes that would suck down escaped convicts to their miserable deaths, certainly contributed to the locating of Dartmoor Prison in Princetown.

Many legends also surround the bodies of water themselves. The Cry of the Dart is a folk tale that suggests that every year the River Dart demands a human life and cries out to summon the victim. Another story tells of Vixiana the witch, who would conjure up thick mists to disorientate travellers before calling out to them and leading them into a mire where a slow and grisly death was waiting. Gaze into the waters of Crazywell Pool on Midsummer's Eve and you will see the likeness of the next parishioner to die, while Bloody Pool on the south east edge of the moor is said to sometimes turn red with the blood of warriors slain there.

It is of course the rivers that give life to the gorse, ferns, heather and bracken found in the wildest areas of the moors, and to the oaks ('Dart' means 'oak grown stream'), hazel, holly, rowan and mosses. From birds and lizards to insects and snakes, all are drawn to the delicious damp of the moor, while the grazing sheep, the Devon Red Ruby cattle and the spirited Dartmoor ponies are never far from a source of drinking water.

Floating down a lazy river as the sun flickers teasingly through the branches of the oak trees above you, you may be lucky enough to spot heron or otters. Silently flip your body over and you may be fortunate to see salmon and trout as they swim below you, glimpsed through the beer-bottle peaty brown of the water. It's a desire to relax by a rippling stream or playful river that attracts millions of picnicking families each year to one of the last great wildernesses in the UK.

Of course all this water has to come from somewhere and a popular saying goes "If you can see the moors clearly, it's going to rain. If

Tavy Cleave, Dartmoor

West Dart, nr Scorhill

Sharrah Pool, River Dart

All of this wetness has created the most wonderful natural playground and health spa for wild swimmers. There are old flooded quarries where nature has reclaimed the scarred remains of industrial plundering. Rivers provide marvellous dipping and infinity pools, sliding rocks and Cresta Runs. There are long lazy stretches, perfect for laps before drying on a sunny rock. There are invigorating waterfalls and evocative springs, daring rapids and salmon leaps. Dartmoor is water, and water is life.

EARLY ADVENTURERS

The Victorians were really the first to see Dartmoor as anything other than a bleak place to be avoided, or at best, endured. People started to have the leisure time to explore, and guide books started to appear. One of the earliest was by William Crossing, published in 1888, with the delightful title, *Amid Devonia's Alps*. He later produced his famous *Guide to Dartmoor*. Since then many hundreds, if not thousands, of books have appeared, but there are certain classics that we use frequently. One is *A Perambulation of Dartmoor* by Samuel Rowe, first published in 1848, a delightful account of fifteen excursions, with particularly florid and romantic descriptions.

you can't, it already is." The higher areas of the moors seem to act like a giant sponge for all of this rainwater, and remarkably all of Devon's main rivers originate within a short stroll of each other, close to Cranmere Pool, before heading to their final destinations on opposite coasts.

Beneath the brow of moorland tors
Slow winds her rivers to the sea
And echoes of the past come down
Deep valley veiled in mystery

A Dartmoor Idyll by Joseph Pears

It's a wet old place indeed and one rather wonderful tale tells of a young man walking past a bog and spotting a hat on the ground. Picking it up, he is startled to find a man's head underneath. At once he offers to help pull the man from the mire, only to hear that the gentleman needs help rescuing the horse he is sitting on as well.

In the 1950s, after the creation of the National Parks, *Dartmoor* by Hansford Worth, another classic book, was published posthumously. Rather than describing itineraries, it is divided by themes. For example there are chapters on stone rows, place names and hut circles. Another brilliant book, though it is a veritable tome at over a thousand pages, is *High Dartmoor* by Eric Hemery, published in 1983. It describes Dartmoor in great detail, with chapters organised according to the moor's rivers. Although it can be difficult to follow, his scholarship and knowledge of Dartmoor is inspiring; the book also has a very useful glossary of Dartmoor terms.

SOUTH DEVON

When Adam and Eve were dispossess'd
Of the Garden hard by Heaven,
They planted another one down in the West,
'Twas Devon, 'twas Devon, glorious Devon.

Old England's counties by the sea
From east to west are seven;
But the gem of that fair galaxy
Is Devon, is Devon, glorious Devon.

From Glorious Devon by Sir Edward German

Think of the South Devon coast, and adventure springs to mind. For centuries pirates, smugglers and fishermen held sway over this rugged, craggy shore, taking advantage of its secluded caves and secret coves. Ancient traders were wrecked as they made their way along the English Channel, sailing too close to the treacherous rocks, and gold coins can still be found from a Spanish Armada hospital ship which was wrecked near Hope Cove. Villagers would go to the high vantage points on the cliffs and watch for shoals of pilchard, which would then be caught in their millions by courageous fishermen, who ventured out to sea in tiny wooden boats.

The amazing history of this part of Devon is, in many ways subtle and hidden. A rusting metal ring stuck into the side of a rock on a beach may indicate an old landing place, or perhaps where a

Elberry Cove, Paignton

Start Bay, from Start Point

Both: Great Mattiscombe Sand

fisherman strung out his pots. A cave set deep into the cliff may well have been used by smugglers; an unobtrusive brick structure, as a lookout post during times of war. And in some places you can see little ancient steps carved into the rock; but who used them remains a mystery.

South Devon is largely unspoilt and breathtakingly beautiful. The towns of Torquay, Paignton and Brixham form the largest urban area, then there are the ancient market towns of Totnes and Newton Abbot, and the bustling coastal communities of Dartmouth and Kingsbridge. In between is a rural idyll – the curve of fertile green hillsides and ploughed red earth fields, dotted with working farms and thatched villages. A particularly special characteristic of South Devon is its beautiful estuaries; the Teign, the Dart, the Avon, the Erme and the Yealm, all of which rise on Dartmoor and weave their course down to the sea. The final estuary in Kingsbridge is not in fact a river at all, but a ria, or drowned valley.

South Devon has bred more than its fair share of brave adventurers, setting off from our shores to discover the world. Some of history's great explorers hailed from South Devon, including the Elizabethan Sir Humphrey Gilbert, who was born at Greenway House near Brixham, learned his seamanship skills on the River Dart, and went on to claim Newfoundland for the English crown. Or Percy Fawcett, born in Torquay, who is said to be the inspiration of both Indiana Jones and Sir Arthur Conan Doyle's dinosaur adventure, *The Lost World*.

The Victorians discovered Torquay as a resort, when swimming became fashionable and people flocked to the coast. Torquay was particularly popular because of its mild climate and huge, sheltered bay with shallow, usually calm water – attributes which are still enjoyed today. Brunel's incredible feats of engineering carried these early tourists along the beautiful stretch of railway between Dawlish and Teignmouth and over the

Soar Mill Cove

remarkable viaducts at Broadsands in Paignton. But the rest of South Devon's stunning coast remained largely undiscovered to the wider world until the 20th century, when smart hotels started to be built, most notably at Burgh Island and at Gara Rock, near Salcombe. Rich people built holiday homes, or bought old houses as holiday retreats. Two of the most notable were the D'Oyly Cartes, who created an Art Deco masterpiece at Coleton Fishacre in the 1920s, and of course Agatha Christie, who bought Greenway, by the River Dart, in 1938. Sailing enthusiasts flocked to Dartmouth and Salcombe, and gradually the world started to notice the dramatic, unspoilt South Devon coast.

The swim walks in this section of the book will take you to some remarkable places, with the excitement increased by the variables of the tide, the weather and the seasons. The rivers and estuaries make beautiful swimming spots, as do the hundreds of coves and beaches, some secluded and deserted, others bustling with holidaying families enjoying this stunning stretch of coast. And with each swim walk, you'll discover more about the astonishing history and heritage of this stretch of coast and the extraordinary people entwined in its story.

RIGHTS AND RESPONSIBILITIES

*S*adly some people want to blame walkers and swimmers for increased littering in wild spots, or claim that we have a negative effect on delicate eco-systems. This has certainly been the case with some swim spots on Dartmoor. With this in mind we've created a wild swimmers' code, not because these accusations are true, but to show that we are some of the most environmentally aware people enjoying these beauty spots. It's common sense to all of us, but if we leave no trace and take away more litter than we came with, these accusations can no longer be aimed at us. We've also only included walks and swims that are accessible from public footpaths and land, as while we are real advocates for access to swim spots and walking routes, we don't want to escalate any existing tensions. Indeed the question of where you can swim – particularly on Dartmoor - is pretty complex. Over half of Dartmoor National Park (57%) is privately owned, mostly by the Duchy of Cornwall. The rest is owned by the Ministry of Defence, the National Trust, the Forestry Commission, water companies and the national park authority. And while much of Dartmoor was designated as access land thanks to the Dartmoor Commons Act of 1985, this doesn't necessarily apply to wild swimming.

Dartmoor National Park Authority welcomes responsible swimmers (believing that no single recreational activity is more important than another), but this isn't always the case with landowners. Many have understandable and genuine concerns about safety and environmental damage. In fact one landowner has become so upset by the amounts of rubbish that he's started blocking off car parks by the River Dart. Our continued freedom of access requires a responsible approach by all, as it could so easily be lost.

With this in mind we have created a Wild Swimming code:

THE WILD SWIMMING CODE

• Car share whenever possible and park sensibly, without blocking roads, turning places or gateways.

• Do not leave litter, and pick up any rubbish that you find.

• Do nothing to damage the ecosystem, from feeding ponies to removing anything besides rubbish.

• In the autumn and winter, on Dartmoor's rivers, do not tread in the fine gravel as this is where salmon and sea trout lay their eggs.

• Don't light fires, including disposable barbecues.

• Respect other water users including fishermen and canoeists/kayakers.

• Leave only footprints, take only memories.

Peartree Point

Tavy Cleave

WILD SWIMMING SAFETY

Great Mattiscombe Sand

Take extra care following heavy rainfall, when rivers might be in spate and flowing much faster than normal.

Watch out in high surf - rip-currents can form which take you out to sea, to behind the breaking waves. Swim perpendicularly from them to escape, then body-surf back in.

Beware of tidal currents, especially near estuary mouths and around headlands, especially at mid-tide, and on fortnightly spring tides, when flows are strongest.

If you are concerned about water quality, cover cuts and open wounds with plasters and do not swim front crawl.

TIDES AND WEATHER CONDITIONS FOR SOUTH DEVON

When planning a swim on the South Devon coast, it's very useful to look at the wind forecast as well as the tides. If you want calm water, you need to know which way the wind is coming from. The prevailing winds in Devon are south westerly, and if this is the case, then choose a swim spot that faces east. Conversely, if the winds are easterly, then it's a good idea to pick a west or south west facing beach. The principle here is that you don't want the wind blowing from the sea onto the land, as the sea is more likely to be rough. Tides are of course very important. Before you go, find out what the tide is doing; it is important to know whether it's going out or coming in. The interesting thing to note about tides in South Devon is that on spring tides (the biggest tides, occurring at the time of the full and new moons), high water will always be at about 6pm, while low water will always be at about noon.

Plan your walk, taking necessary supplies and protection; don't forget water, a map, compass and waterproofs, especially on the moor.

Remember that cold water can limit your swimming endurance. If it is your first outdoor swim of the season, be careful to enter the water slowly and acclimatise. Stay close to the shore until you are comfortable. Wear a wetsuit for added warmth and buoyancy. Do not overestimate your ability. Remember that the cold water quickly creates hypothermia – shivering is the first stage.

Don't enter water without first establishing an exit point, especially in fast-flowing water. Never jump or dive into water without first checking the depth and whether there are any obstructions. Even if you have jumped/dived there before, always check every time. Large obstructions like tree branches and rocks move about underwater and an area that was previously clear may well be blocked.

Swim in a group wherever possible or, if swimming alone, let people know your movements and take extra special care.

PRACTICALITIES

The Ordnance Survey 1:25,000 Explorer maps of Dartmoor and South Devon are essential. There is the traditional orange folded map, and the very handy book form: the *A-Z's Dartmoor Adventure Atlas* and the *A-Z's South West Coast Path Adventure Atlas*. You can also see OS mapping for free on a desktop computer at home (does not work on mobile phones or tablets), using Bing Maps. You can print these maps and some people make 'screen grabs' of the appropriate section and save them or email them to view later on their phones. You can also buy OS maps for your phone using a range of apps such as Memory-Map and View-ranger. We give directions for all the walks and swims, doing our best to describe the route, but it's important to realise that Dartmoor in particular is a wilderness and you cannot rely on written directions alone, particularly for some of the more remote swims and walks (of which there are many). A map is vital and a compass is also very useful.

DOWNLOADABLE route information, to print out or to transfer to your smart phone, can be found at wildthingspublishing.com/dartmoor. Insert the last two words of each chapter introduction, with no spaces or capitals. E.g. for Walk 1 go to wildthingspublishing.com/dartmoor/pleasurableexperience.

Coastpath near Dartmouth

River Dart, Holne Bridge

FURTHER INSPIRATION

Several websites have been invaluable in compiling this book and we would encourage you to visit them for even more tips and inspiration. The South West Coast Path website (southwestcoastpath.org.uk) was brilliant for suggested routes and in-depth information. Several of the swim walks take in National Trust properties and managed land and beaches and their website (nationaltrust.org.uk) is packed with ideas for great days out.

Devon Wild Swimming is an informal gathering of mainly weekend walkers and swimmers and is a great way to join an adventure, though you do so at your own risk. To find out where to swim, and who to swim with visit:

www.devonandcornwallwildswimming.co.uk
www.facebook.com/groups/devonwildswimming

There are various organised swims every year too.

Swims in Torbay - www.geoparkadventure.com
Dart 10K and Bantham Swoosh - www.outdoorswimmingsociety.com
Topsham to Turf swim - www.estuary-league-of-friends.co.uk
Breakwater Swim, Plymouth - www.chestnutappeal.org.uk
Burgh Island - www.swimtrek.com
Swim tours - www.devonshiredippers.com
Agatha Christie Swim in Paignton - www.daat.org
Swims in Brixham and Plymouth- www.thebluemile.com

Devon wild swimmer Chris Popham has put together a really comprehensive swimming map of Devon at https://goo.gl/ATfs4O and you can also search the map at www.wildswimming.co.uk

Tavy Cleave

Sharrah Pool, River Dart

Dartmoor

Walk 1

WEST OKEMENT AND MELDON CIRCULAR

Plunge in a mountain waterfall pool, hike up to see the highest points of Dartmoor, and finish with a swim in a large green lake.

INFORMATION

This walk is best done in summer as it can be boggy. The terrain is high so in misty weather it is easy to get lost.

DISTANCE: 5 miles
TIME: 5 hours
MAP: OS Explorer Dartmoor OL28
START POINT: Meldon Reservoir car park (SX 561 917, EX20 4LU)
END POINT: Meldon Reservoir car park
PUBLIC TRANSPORT: Bus or train to Okehampton, then travel by taxi to Meldon Reservoir
SWIMMING: Pools and waterfalls on the West Okement (SX 559 900), and large quarry lake at Meldon Pond (SX 563 921)
PLACES OF INTEREST: West Okement River, Black-a-Tor Copse ancient woodland
REFRESHMENTS: There are lots of cafés and pubs in Okehampton, including Toast Coffee House, in the old Edwardian cinema, which has free wifi (01837 54494, EX20 1HN). There is also the Bearslake Inn in nearby Sourton, in a beautiful thatched Devon longhouse (01837 861334, EX20 4HQ).

The walk starts at Meldon Reservoir, which certainly divides opinion. It was opened in 1974, and involved the destruction of the lower part of the West Okement gorge which caused huge controversy at the time, especially as Dartmoor had only recently become a National Park. One Dartmoor blogger, John Bainbridge, who has now sadly left the area, doesn't mince his words, describing how a "magnificent valley" was lost, he claims, "as a result of a short-term solution to Devon's water-shortage, and promoted by local jobsworths who seemed to have a real hatred of the National Park". However Eric Hemery, in *High Dartmoor*, describes the reservoir as "serpentine" and a place of "stern, almost classical beauty".

You arrive at Vellake Corner ❸, a marshy plain which has an interesting array of boggy plants, including Dartmoor's answer to the venus fly trap, the carnivorous sundew plant, which eats insects, and is incredibly rare. You will also see bog asphodel, which has a bright yellow flower. If you don't mind getting a bit damp, get down on your knees and look at the plants close up; it is a fascinating world in miniature. These plants are best seen between June and August.

The walk then proceeds up beside the West Okement River which bubbles, tumbles and rushes down the hillside. This part of the river is traditionally known as the Valley of the Rocks and some of the boulders are truly enormous. They have undoubtedly been moved around in violent storms over the last millennia; the force of the water is an awesome thought. Just before the brow of the hill, when you see an oak tree on the left ❹, there is a great plunge pool with two waterfalls. Scramble down to the right of the path, and you will find the pool. It's surprisingly deep under the main waterfall where you can brace yourself against the moss-lined rock for a vigorous pummelling. There is also an intriguing 'indoor' waterfall next to it, in a niche formed from several large boulders. It even has 'windows'! This is a great place to stop for a dip and a picnic.

After your dip, as you continue along the path, you pass a tree with a big round growth into which someone has carved a smiley face. You pass around the left side of a wall enclosing a weir, and are out in open country again, with magnificent Corn Ridge up ahead to the right, and Shelstone Tor looming over the Valley of the Rocks. Corn Ridge is the part of the walk that feels like the Lake District; it's a proper mountainside. Look out for the Slipper Stones on the side of the ridge (they are marked on the OS map). These are large areas of granite, exposed by the constant passage of water down the hillside. Why they are called the Slipper Stones is not clear. William Crossing, who wrote a famous guide to Dartmoor, believes one looks like a large slipper, while Hansford Worth, another well-known authority on Dartmoor, believes the name is a corruption of 'Slippery Stones'. Eric Hemery describes them rather beautifully as "shining when wet like a giant skylight on the hillside".

The next point of interest is Black-a-Tor Copse ❺, one of three ancient oak woodlands on Dartmoor (the others are Wistman's Wood and Piles Copse). This is the highest of the three. Here's what Worth has to say about them: "All these woods are so exceptional in their main characteristics as to be unique, not only in Britain but also probably in the whole world. They are remarkable, not for luxuriant tree growth or great extent, but for their diminutive trees and extremely limited areas; while the excessive

humidity of the region in which they exist and other extraordinary conditions amid which they grow can only be described as weird."

It's thought that these three dwarf oak woods are the ancient remains of forests which could date back many thousands of years. Most of the forests were destroyed by prehistoric people in the Bronze Age, when they started to clear land for farming and settlement. Black-a-Tor Copse, or to give its old name, Black-a-Tor Beare, contains many species of mosses, ferns and lichens, and is a wonderful place to sit and let the mind wander back to ancient times. There is certainly a mystical air, and you could well start to dream about the woods being populated with Druids and pixies.

Black Tor ❻ is the next stop. It's a hard steep climb up to the top, but it is worth the hike. Give yourself a pat on the back when you reach the summit, as you've climbed virtually to the top of Dartmoor. Over to the north east (the opposite direction from Black-a-Tor copse) you can see High Willhays, at 621 metres the highest point on the moor, and then to the left of it is Yes Tor. Military huts and red-and-white markers for the Okehampton firing range are also visible.

Looking the other way, back down over Black-a-Tor Copse, is an equally spectacular view, starting with Branscombe's Loaf on the top of Corn Ridge, a small squat tor like a pimple on the horizon. Moving along to the right, you will then see Sourton Tor, with three outcrops, and Shelstone Tor, above the Valley of the Rocks. You also get the chance for another good look at the Slipper Stones.

Branscombe's Loaf is named after a medieval Bishop, who got lost while travelling on Dartmoor. Tired and hungry, he came across a stranger who offered him bread and cheese, if he

would only get off his horse, doff his cap and call him master. He was about to accept gratefully, when his sharp-eyed chaplain noticed the stranger had a cloven hoof. The Bishop cried out to God and made the sign of the cross, whereupon the stranger vanished and the bread and cheese was turned to stone – and remains on the top of Corn Ridge to this day!

From Black Tor the walk continues directly north along a track, heading downwards. From here the counties of Cornwall and Devon spread ahead of you, a spectacular view that stretches for miles. The track takes you down to the old site of Meldon Quarry, with the very pretty Red-a-ven Brook running through it. The quarry was created in Victorian times to mine stone for the railway industry, and is now mothballed. The lake ❽, or as it's often known, Old Meldon Pond, is absolutely beautiful. Above it towers the magnificent Meldon Viaduct, built in the 1870s to carry the railway. It's now home to the Granite Way cycle track.

We first visited the lake on a winter's day and were entranced; it was an enticing slate-green expanse, glimpsed through a network of branches. There is a beautiful, angular cliff hanging precariously over the water. It's one of those places where the colours constantly change, according to the sky, the season, and the amount of leaves on the trees. In the winter, it has a stark, grey beauty; in the summer it's a lush green oasis. It is a truly amazing place to swim, but one thing to be aware of is glass around the edges; it's a bit of a party hangout on summer evenings, so litter can be a hazard. Whenever we've visited it's been empty, and the sheer freedom of swimming in such a vast pool of water is a memorable and very pleasurable experience.

DIRECTIONS

1 From the car park, cross the dam and turn right, following the path with the reservoir on your right.
0.4 miles

2 By a gate, marked Meldon Reservoir, keep on the main path and follow it as it bears left, crossing a footbridge and continuing on around the reservoir until you reach a wide marshy area called Vellake Corner.
0.8 miles

3 From here, follow the path to the left of the open area, with the West Okement River on your right, and follow it uphill.
0.5 miles

4 Just before the brow of the hill, you will see an oak tree on the left. You can scramble down here to the right of the path for a dip in the waterfall and pool below. Continue along the path and follow it to the left around a crenellated walled off area (which encloses a weir). Continue to follow the path to Black-a Tor Copse.
0.5 miles

5 Explore the copse and then retrace your steps to the beginning of the copse. Turn right to climb up to the top of Black Tor which is behind the copse.
0.2 miles

6 From the top of Black Tor, look north and you will see a track into the distance. Take this track. Following the track, you pass a flagpole for the military firing range on your left. The track starts to descend and you can see a quarry ahead. The track then curves downwards to the left.
1.5 miles

7 Take the first path off to the right. The path hairpins down to the bottom; just keep on the path and it will bring you out by Red-a-ven Brook. Cross the brook via the bridge, turn left and follow the path towards Meldon Pond. You get to a fork in the path; keep left and follow the path to a clam bridge which takes you across Red-a-Ven brook again and to the Pond.
0.6 miles

8 From Meldon Pond, to get back to the car park, walk back past the clam bridge, keeping the river on your left, and the path takes you up hill back to the car park.
0.3 miles

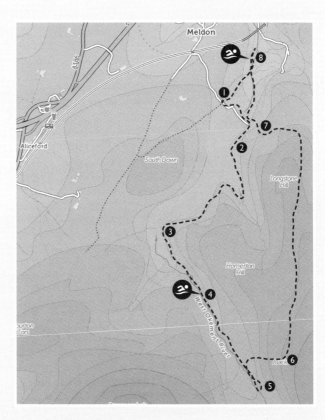

31

Walk 2

EAST OKEMENT POOLS AND TAW MARSH CIRCULAR

An epic walk, taking you from ancient woodland and up to the stark heights of the moor with beautiful waterfalls and pools.

*Y*ou start on the edge of Okehampton, underneath a handsome stone viaduct, built in the 1870s, which used to carry the main trains between Plymouth and Waterloo. Not quite so handsome is the road bridge carrying the A30, which thunders overhead. You then walk beside the river, which is like a wonderful watery staircase. It gurgles down a series of drops of varying shapes and sizes and is packed with pools and waterfalls. This stretch is known as West Cleave, and is surrounded by ancient woods.

The map-maker Samuel Rowe, in his classic work of 1848 *A Perambulation of Dartmoor* describes it as follows: "The course of the river through this secluded glen presents a succession of scenes of romantic grandeur and wild magnificence. The river comes foaming down from the moors over a solid granite bed, in some places sufficiently steep to form a succession of waterfalls, and makes its way through a deep mountain gorge."

Particularly notable are West Cleave Rocks (an unusual horizontal mass of rock like a pavement), and a little further up there is a spectacular, twenty foot high waterfall ❸, which is one of the best places to stop and swim. Make a base at the top of the waterfall and you can swim in a large pool above it, with cascades at the top. You can then climb down to the pool below the waterfall and swim there – an exhilarating experience because of the sheer energy buzzing from the waterfall.

After your swim you leave the woodland and head out onto the open moor. Walking south you see the river making its way into the distance on your right. Don't miss the Nine Maidens stone circle ❺, which has a wonderfully intimate feel because it is particularly small. There are actually a lot more than nine stones, and the traditional myth is that they represent nine young women who were turned to stone after going dancing instead of attending church. But in fact, in

INFORMATION

DISTANCE: 7 miles
TIME: 5 hours
MAP: OS Explorer Dartmoor OL28
START POINT: Fatherford. Park by the side of road at SX 603 948, EX20 1QG. From the centre of Okehampton take the B3260 East and then turn right down Fatherford Road. At the bottom turn right. The road comes to a dead end and there is a parking area on the right. The walk strays into a small part of the Okehampton firing range so check there's no firing before you go: www.gov.uk/government/publications/dartmoor-firing-programme
END POINT: Fatherford
PUBLIC TRANSPORT: Trains from Exeter to Okehampton and plenty of buses to Okehampton. Then a half hour walk out of Okehampton to the start point
SWIMMING: Pools and waterfalls on the East Okement, particularly at the large waterfall (SX 607 936), large pool at Taw Marsh (SX 619 914)
PLACES OF INTEREST: East Okement River, West Cleave Rocks, Nine Maidens Stone Circle, Cullever Steps, Irishman's Wall, Taw Marsh.
REFRESHMENTS: The Tors pub at Belstone is the only place that serves food and drink on the walk. It's a fairly basic pub where you can get simple food and refreshments (01837 840689, EX20 1QZ).

cultures across the world, there are many stories about nine women, going back to pre-Christian times. For example the Nine Muses or the Nine Valkyries. One writer, Ruth St Leger-Gordon, believed the concept went back to witches worshipping the moon in three phases: crescent, full and waning, with each phase being represented by a lunar goddess. These three phases were again separated into three, giving nine moon goddesses or maidens. This theory could also explain why the 'Nine Maidens' name is often found at sacred places such as groups of trees or wishing wells.

You then head down to Cullever Steps ❼, an ancient ford. There's a beautiful plunge pool in the stream a few hundred metres downstream, just below Scarey Tor. You are now in the Okehampton firing area. The army have been using Dartmoor for training for around two hundred years. It's particularly suitable for marines, paratroopers and infantry, as well as other forces that move mainly on foot. You may well see them training, as the public aren't excluded when they're firing blanks. We once witnessed a training exercise here involving explosions and gunfire, which was particularly exciting for the younger members of the party.

The walk then takes you up and over the hill into the next valley. Walking up from Cullever Steps note Irishman's Wall straight ahead of you. Legend has it that an Irishman came here during the famine and decided he wanted to keep stock on Dartmoor, and so built a wall not knowing that enclosing the commons was not allowed. The locals took great pleasure in letting him build it and then, once it was up, removing most of it overnight.

At the crest of the hill, stop and admire Higher Tor on your left and Winter Tor on your right. As you descend into the next valley you can see the River Taw at the bottom. This valley feels bleakly beautiful: it is stark, and the landscape is smooth and unpunctu-

ated by tors. It feels as though you have crossed into foreign territory, perhaps into the wilds of somewhere remote like Afghanistan. At the bottom you reach the area known as Taw Marsh ❾. There is a crossing point with a ford, and this is the next swimming spot.

There is a large pool on the bend just upstream from the ford. We've christened it 'Ophelia's Pool', as there are beautiful long green weeds, like hair, all flowing downstream, as in the famous painting by John Everett Millais. You can swim here and then go upstream as the river narrows. The water isn't very deep and at times it feels a bit like bog snorkelling, but it is actually very magical. You swim along, nose level with the reeds, flowers and sphagnum moss, totally immersed in the microcosm of the river, looking up to the majestic mountain of Steeperton Tor straight ahead of you. Sphagnum moss is found frequently on Dartmoor, and it was collected during the First World War to provide dressings for wounded soldiers because of its natural antiseptic and absorbent qualities.

The next part of the walk takes you north towards Belstone, but don't miss some extraordinary twentieth century remains just off to the right of the path. You'll see what looks like a bunker with Keep Out signs, and glass and metal hatches on the ground. These are the remains of an unsuccessful attempt in the 1950s by the North Devon Water Board to sink trial boreholes to see if there might be an underground lake. Water was found but it turned out to be radioactive and the project came to nought.

You then reach the picturesque village of Belstone ❿, which despite appearing lost in the mists of time has its own Twitter account. Look out for the unusual old Zion Chapel with its Telegraph Office sign. There's a pub, The Tors, where you can stop for a well-earned rest, before making your way down through fields back to where you started.

❶ Leave the car at Fatherford and walk towards the viaduct. Go through the gate and cross the wooden bridge over the river, admiring the viaduct overhead.
0.1 miles

❷ Turn left after the bridge and follow the path up the river, with the river on your left. Keep following the path uphill, over a clam bridge and through a gap in the wall. You will pass lots of cascades.
0.4 miles

❸ The path then gets steeper with a hand rail on the left. Notice the large waterfall on the left. This is the first swimming spot – there is a big pool above the large waterfall, and numerous other pools.
0.2 miles

❹ Carry on walking with the river on your left. You come to another clam bridge over the river (there is also a ford and stepping stones). Cross the bridge and note the dramatic blasted tree. This is a good place for a picnic.
0.1 miles

❺ Turn right and follow the path with the river on your right, and keep following it up the side of the hill. The path meets a military track. Cross the track, and another one, and head uphill. You will see Belstone Tor ahead. Bear slightly left to visit the Nine Maidens stone circle.
0.6 miles

6 From the circle take the path south, and then bear right and pick up the military track. You reach a junction of paths. Turn right here to get to Cullever Steps (there is also another swimming opportunity at a pool downstream below Scarey Tor).
0.6 miles

7 From Cullever Steps go back to the junction and, heading south, take the left fork. You will see Irishman's Wall to the left. Ahead is Higher Tor and to the right is Winter Tor. Turn left by the boundary stone marked WD. The path meets a rocky track which you follow uphill, bending to the right. It takes you around the hill, and at the crest you pass between Higher Tor on the left and Winter Tor on the right. Looking at Winter Tor you have the spectacle of, left to right, High Willhays, Yes Tor and Rowtor.
0.6 miles

8 At the next fork you turn left. Note group of boundary stones on the left. Walk down the hill. Make your way down an indistinct path to Taw Marsh.
0.8 miles

9 After swimming, with your back to the pool, take the track to the left, and then cross the rough ground to pick up the track going north to Belstone. Walk with the river on the right. This track takes you all the way to the village.
0.9 miles

10 Walk into the village where you will find the Tors pub on your left.

Carry on past it and turn left at the old Zion Chapel, and then take the lane on the right. Don't go down the road marked Dead End. Follow the lane past old Rectory Farm on the left, until you get to a cattle grid.
0.9 miles

11 Take the public footpath on the left signed to Fatherford, and follow the path through the fields until you get to a stream which you cross over a little granite bridge. You then get to another lane. Turn left here, go under the A30 road bridge, and then under the Fatherford railway bridge. Turn left immediately after the bridge and you will see the parking area on the right.
0.8 miles

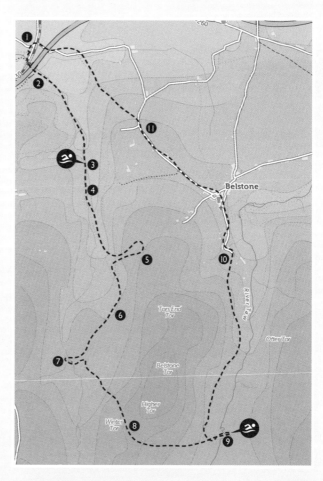

Walk 3

SHILLEY POOL CIRCULAR

Walk up onto the open moors with glorious views across northern Devon, discover a remarkable triple stone row, and swim in a magical pool.

INFORMATION

DISTANCE: 4.5 miles
TIME: 4-5 hours
MAP: OS Explorer Dartmoor OL28
START POINT: South Zeal Car Park (SX 651 934, EX20 2JZ)
END POINT: South Zeal Car Park
PUBLIC TRANSPORT: The 178 runs between Newton Abbot and Okehampton via South Zeal.
SWIMMING: Shilley Pool, Blackaton Brook (SX 652 912)
PLACES OF INTEREST: South Zeal, Cosdon triple stone row
REFRESHMENTS: The Oxenham Arms is the oldest heritage inn in Devon and Cornwall, with low beams, flagged floors and mullioned windows, as well as a garden with great views across the moors (01837 840244, EX20 2JT). The thatched Kings Arms is a 14th century village local pub, serving real ales, farm cider and hearty homemade fare (01837 840300, EX20 2JP).

The walk starts in the pretty medieval village of South Zeal ❶, home to the Dartmoor Folk Festival for almost 40 years. It's a lively little place and has been since the 13th century when it was a popular stop on a trade route between Exeter and Okehampton, and on to Cornwall. The spinning and weaving of sheep's wool had become a popular cottage industry here by the 18th century (look out for the clues in local names like Tucking Mill Field and the adjacent Washing Place). Later, in the 19th century, South Zeal housed tin miners. Indeed there were so many migrant workers employed at Ramsley Copper Mine (on the hill above the village) it gained the nickname Irishman's Town. At the time the town had its own bakers, shoemakers, tailors and milliners, as well as a selection of general stores and five pubs.

Strolling around the village today you'll discover St Mary's Chapel, which was once the home of the village school for nearly 200 years. You'll also spot the Market Cross at the end of the churchyard, which was erected as a tribute to the village's medieval market, established by charter in 1298. It's also worth popping your head into the Country Store and Tea Room, a charming old shop and the perfect place to pick up some supplies for the walk.

Opposite you'll find one of the village's two pubs, The Oxenham Arms, a former coaching inn dating back to the 12th century and a monastery before that. In one of the rooms you'll discover a prehistoric standing stone in one of the walls – the original monastery was built around it. The pub can also claim some impressive guests including Charles Dickens, who stayed here while writing the Pickwick Papers, as well as Francis Drake, Admiral Nelson, David Bowie and the Rolling Stones. The pub also pops up in Charles's Kingsley's *Westward Ho!*, which references the legend of a white-breasted bird whose appearance was said to foretell a death in the Oxenham family who once lived here. 'The Ox' is also said to be haunted by both a monk and a lady.

The Dartmoor Way passes through the garden of the pub, although our walk takes you up onto the colossal Cosdon Hill, which at 550m high dominates the north east side of Dartmoor and was once believed to be the highest point on Dartmoor. That honour actually goes to its neighbour, High Willhays which is a full 71m higher. It's not the size of the hill, but what you discover when you climb it, and there are some real treats in store. The walk takes you on bridleways and tracks up onto the moor, which boast glorious views over northern Devon. Look out for Castle Drogo in the distance when you first get out onto the open moor.

Cosdon Hill was once used as a beacon (with its nearest neighbour being Dunkery on Exmoor), with fires lit in times of danger and celebration on the summit of its natural dome. It's easy to imagine a chain of beacons being lit across the region at the threat of the approaching Spanish Armada. The most impressive evidence of human activity on the hillside is the incredible triple stone row ❹, known locally as The Cemetery and dating back at least to the Bronze Age. The row runs uphill to a ruined cairn and even features a pair of burial kists. The wonderful Legendary Dartmoor website (legendarydartmoor.co.uk) suggests that,

because they are joined by a common end slab, they could very well be a 'his and hers' grave. We've noticed that these Neolithic monuments on the moor always seem to attract curious numbers of wild animals. Are they drawn by some powerful mystical force or because they are constructed on ley lines? Or perhaps because they make excellent scratching posts? Whatever the history of the special spot, it makes a lovely place to relax and take in the peace of the moors and the outstanding views. We like this wonderful poem about Cosdon Hill, which has also been known as Cawsand in the past…

On Cawsand Beacon

Rolling o'er the purple heather,
In the glorious Summer weather,
Staining lips with whortleberries,
Sweet as any figs or cherries.

Sipping from the crystal stream,
Lying on the banks to dream,
Watching skylarks soar above
Singing, with them, strains of love.

Gazing o'er yon boundless plain,
List'ning to the sweet refrain
Of the rivulets and rills
As they flow by distant hills;

Hearing voices, strange and low,
Mystic tones that come and go,
Seeing tors salute each other,
Every one a friend and brother.

Elias Tozer - 1873

When you are ready to make your way to one of these crystal streams, head towards the valley, looking out for evidence of an ancient hut circle along the way. It's always fun finding a spot to cross Blackaton Brook, looking for suitable stepping stones or a place where you can make a leap of faith. Then find the path that winds its way down through the gorse-covered valley, following the stream from above. You can't miss Shilley Pool ❺, which is so idyllic it looks as though it could have been constructed by Hollywood set builders in the early days of technicolor. It's the perfect aquatic playground, with smooth slabs of rock forming a natural waterslide for splashing down into the near-circular pool, before swimming to the lower end, dammed by boulders to form an infinity pool. Only around a metre deep, it's still perfect for a dip, before drying off on one of the many flat slabs nearby.

Suitably refreshed, continue down through the valley and onto the lane. It's then a really pleasant walk past farm buildings and cottages with produce for sale by honesty boxes, back into South Zeal. You could pop into 'The Ox' for a well-deserved pint, although it's also worth considering the other pub in town, The Kings Arms, which is a mere baby in comparison at only around 500 years old. They have camping and host a variety of events including the annual limerick competition, read by independent performers to preserve the author's anonymity. While enjoying a pint, why not have a go? We'll start you off. There was a young man called Billy, who went for a walk up to Shilley...

DIRECTIONS

① Walk back out of the car park and turn left and left again onto the High Street. Turn left just before The Mill House and walk through some old farm buildings and then out through the granite gates. Bear left across the fields following the hedge and then through the kissing gate. Turn right up the lane and walk past the red phone box, crossing straight over the road at the stop sign and onto the track signed Bridlepath to the Moor.
0.4 miles

② Continue up the hill, turning left at the Public Bridleway sign onto a walled track and past the three steps built into a wall, onto a dual concrete farm track. Follow around to the left and along a high walled path past a sign for Pixie Garden. Carry straight on at the fork following the sign for Cawsand and the Moor. At the next fork take the right through the wooden gate marked Public Bridleway. Go left at the next fork and go left of

the gate onto a high-walled path. Go through another gate and over a stream by a granite gate post and onto the moor.
0.7 miles

③ Cross a couple of streams and walking between two walls, turn right where the four gates meet. Keep following the wall to your left until you reach its corner and then bear right following the path up onto the hill. As it begins to plateau, look out for the stone rows, which you should spot to the left of the two trees.
0.6 miles

④ When you are ready to continue, stand at the top looking straight down the stone rows and look for the diagonal path going off to the right south east down towards the valley. Walk past the hut circle and down towards the stream, crossing where you can and then turning left to follow it down the hill. Look out for a stone wall off to the left that pretty much marks Shilley Pool.
1.1 miles

⑤ After your swim follow the track downstream winding back down the hill and to the road. Turn left into the road and follow it back to the village. Eventually turn left by the 30mph and bridge warning sign and then left back into the car park.
1.9 miles

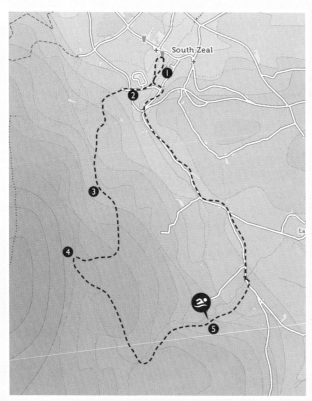

Walk 4

TEIGN GORGE CIRCULAR

This is one of the most popular and scenic walks in Devon, taking you from a hilltop castle and down a spectacular wooden river valley with pools.

Castle Drogo is Britain's newest castle, built in the 1920s by a social climber called Julius Drewe. At the end of the 19th century he made his fortune through importing tea and then branched out into owning one of the UK's most successful retail chains. Rich enough to retire at just 33, he wasn't content to just relax and enjoy the company of his wife and five children and fish to his heart's content, but set about creating his own vanity project.

The well-heeled wannabe found that the aristocracy didn't accept his new-found wealth, so he carried out a 'Who Do You Think You Are' style investigation with his own personal genealogist. The expert found a link between him and the wealthy Drewes of Elizabethan Devon and he even added the extra 'e' to his surname to seal the deal. If that wasn't outrageous enough, the genealogist even managed to find him a family seat by suggesting a vague family link with a 'Dru' or 'Drogo' who had fought alongside William the Conqueror and also a Drogo of Teignton – whom the local village of Drewsteignton was named after. Once he had legally joined the aristocracy, he started building his very own castle, the ultimate in arrogant grand designs.

You'd be hard pushed to buy a Dorset beach hut for £60,000 these days, but the amount of money Julius Drewe pumped into his vanity project back in 1910 would be worth about £40 million today. On his 55th birthday in 1911 he commissioned the renowned architect Edwin Lutyens to build his dream castle. Tragically, Drewe died just a year after his expensive dream was finished in 1930. The next generation of his family found themselves victims of his quirky design. He'd rather foolishly insisted that there were no windowsills or guttering.

INFORMATION

DISTANCE: 4 miles
TIME: 2 hours
MAP: OS Explorer Dartmoor OL28
START POINT: Castle Drogo. Park in the main car park at the castle (SX 725 902, EX6 6PB)
END POINT: Castle Drogo
PUBLIC TRANSPORT: Take the Dartline Coaches Bus 173 from Exeter bus station (passing Exeter Central train station). Operates Monday to Saturday. The bus drops passengers off at the bottom of Castle Drogo's drive
SWIMMING: Drogo Weir/Salmon Leaps (SX 723 897), Fingle Weir (SX 740 898)
PLACES OF INTEREST: Castle Drogo, Drogo Weir and Salmon Leaps, Hydro Electric Plant, Fingle Bridge, Drewsteignton
REFRESHMENTS: Fingle Bridge Inn is a popular riverside pub, well situated for a halfway pit stop (01647 281287, EX6 6PW). The café at Castle Drogo has an outside patio for when the weather's nice (01647 433306, EX6 6PB). The Drewe Arms in Drewsteignton village is a 17th century thatched pub serving real ale and classic pub grub and a choice of accommodation in either four poster beds or a cheaper bunk house (01647 281409, EX6 6QN).

The ridiculous levels of leaks led his heirs to hand over the castle to the National Trust in 1973. During an ambitious five year restoration project, the trust will remove and return 2,355 granite blocks weighing 680 tonnes, and shift entire battlements to allow them to install a new roof the size of two football pitches. They will also be refurbishing more than 900 windows, containing 13,000 panes, to stop them leaking and replacing almost 40 miles of pointing. It's due to be completed in 2017 at a cost of £11 million.

Today's walk takes you from the car park near the castle and winds down into the gorge along Hunter's Path and around Hunter's Tor. The views down into the lush valley as you begin to descend are magnificent and it's easy to understand why Julius Drewe chose this location for his castle. After entering the gorge and walking past the iron bridge you'll come across Drogo Weir ❸, which was built in 1928 to serve the hydroelectric plant just downstream. The 75-metre pool makes a perfect wild swimming spot, shaded by woodland and with a handy metal jetty to enter the water. Watch out for the remains of an old submerged wooden jetty and definitely don't dive in here. Look out for dragonflies and rare water beetles.

The weir serves a double purpose and also helps stock the river with salmon, and Drewe built three impressive cascading pools at the lower end of the weir to allow the upward migration of the spawning salmon. Visit in September or October, when the river is in spate after heavy rains, to see the spectacular sight of them jumping into the weir. It's quite fun to climb into the metre-deep pools (which have smooth concrete bottoms) for a natural jacuzzi. Only attempt this when the river levels are lower, as last time we visited we noticed part of the wall of one of the leaps had been swept

away, which would make it dangerous when the river is flowing fast.

Once you are suitably refreshed, continue the walk downstream along the rocky undulating path, with beautiful views of the river as it winds its way past mossy islands and dipping pools on its way to Teignmouth. See if you can spot the rocking Logan Stone in the riverbed, thought to belong to the Druids. Autumn is a great time to visit, as the woodland takes on its glorious sepia palette, while in spring you can enjoy the carpets of bluebells and daffodils in amongst the hillside bracken.

Look out for the old hydroelectric plant, a Grade II listed building which was also designed by Lutyens. During the early part of the 20th century the castle had no mains electricity and the hydro-electricity plant was installed in the 1920s. It operated right up until 1994, even after Castle Drogo was connected to the National Grid in the late 1950s. It's currently in a state of disrepair, but the National Trust are hoping that the original manufacturer, Gilbert Gilkes, can one day make it fully operational again. You'll also notice the wall of the deer park next to the building.

The path continues alongside oaks once managed by the monks from Buckfast Abbey.

They forced the oaks to grow tall by planting birch in between. The bark would be used for leather tanning, the twigs and branches for charcoal, and the boughs for wood. Originally the trees would be cut down every 25 years as part of the coppicing, to allow new branches to grow from the stumps. Higher up through the woods are oak standards, birch and plantations of conifer. Wild swimming pioneer Roger Deakin talks about a magical stay in a hidden hut in these woods in his delightful book Wildwood.

When the path splits, you have two choices. If the water levels are low you can go over the rocky section that is prone to flooding in the winter months. Otherwise head left, up the steep stone steps and over the rocky outcrop at the foot of Sharp Tor. A little further along the river and through a hunting gate, you'll reach Fingle Weir ❹ and a second chance for a dip. Leave your clothes on Kirsten's Seat bench and enjoy peaty waters shared with salmon, trout and even otters! You can see the remains of a leat that used to supply the Fingle Corn Mill, which burnt down in 1894.

Continuing the walk, the gorge widens and you'll be able to see Prestonbury Castle Iron Age hillfort above Fingle Bridge, facing its dramatic partner, Cranbrook Castle, on the opposite side of the valley. Both were built by the Celts to guard the Teign Valley over 2,000 years before. These days the only invaders are the hordes of tourists who descend on this picturesque spot every summer. The bridge itself was originally a packhorse bridge, built in the 18th century to link Drewsteignton to Moretonhampstead. It replaced the old stepping stones you can still see upstream.

Formerly known as the Anglers' Rest, the Fingle Bridge Inn ❺ started life as a tea shelter founded in 1897 to offer refreshments to fishermen, early tourists and people bringing grain to the mill. You might need some refreshment yourself, before the walk continues up a very steep hill to the top of the valley you have just walked down. Aching calves are a small price to pay for yet more stunning views over the canopy of trees in the deep wooded ravine of the Teign. The Hunter's Path takes you over the top of Sharp Tor and then onto Piddledown Common – a name that children and those of us in our second childhoods still find hilarious.

You can head into Drewsteignton from here, a picturesque village served by the charming thatched Drewe Arms. The pub was originally managed by Mabel Mudge from 1919 until 1994 when she retired at the age of 99, making her the oldest pub landlady in the country. Acclaimed sculptor Peter Randall-Page also lives nearby and you can see several of his works in the village's community garden. Alternatively return to Castle Drogo where one Englishman's home really was his castle. Well, almost.

DIRECTIONS

1 From the car park head onto the road towards the castle and then follow signs for Teign Valley Estate Walks. Follow the sign Hunters Path to Iron Bridge and Chagford. This will take you through a gate and down a hill before you turn right, still following Hunter's Path.
0.6 miles

2 After another gate, the path eventually bends to the left following a stream and signs now say Fisherman's Path. Follow the single track tarmac drive over the cattle grid and stay left at Gib House. Cross the V-shaped stile, and walk past the iron bridge (don't cross it) down to Drew's Weir and pool, and the Salmon Leaps.
0.5 miles

3 Following your swim, follow the river downstream along Fisherman's Path. This beautiful path follows the Teign past the hydroelectric plant on the opposite bank, with a climb up and down the base of Sharp Tor, with some very steep steps.
1.3 miles

4 The path eventually splits into two. The right-hand fork takes you to a second swimming spot created by a weir in the river. Look out for a bench marked Kirsten's Seat. When the water levels are higher there is a small, natural slide down the left of the damn, following the curve in the river's bank. The waters can be quite shallow here in the summer months.
0.2 miles

5 From here it is a short walk continuing along by the river to Fingle Bridge and a stop at the Fingle Bridge Inn for refreshments. Continue on from the pub along the road and car park before turning left following signs for Castle Drogo. This is a very steep climb, which takes you onto Hunter's Path and through a small gate between granite posts (Hunter's Gate) and onto the top of Sharp Tor with spectacular views of the Teign Valley.
1 mile

6 Continue along the path through the gate onto Piddledown Common, along a path lined with gorse, and back to the car park at Castle Drogo.
0.3 miles

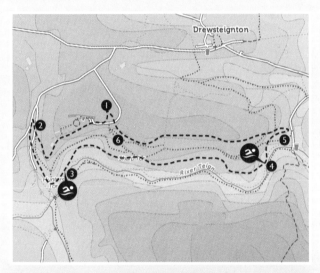

49

KESTOR ROCK, SCORHILL AND GIDLEIGH CIRCULAR

A glorious walk taking in fascinating ancient monuments, including one of the best stone circles on the moor. We cross the lovely North Teign River, with two swimming opportunities.

The walk starts at Batworthy, where large numbers of flint tools have been found, which are thought to date back to the Mesolithic period, 12,000 to 6,500 years ago. As will soon become apparent on the walk, this area of Dartmoor has been occupied by man for many thousands of years.

The first stop is at Kestor Rock ❷, which has an unusual natural basin at the top, full of water. The Victorians were fascinated by the basin, believing it was the focus of ancient Druidical ceremonies, with some quite gruesome ideas about it being used to collect blood from human sacrifices. It's about three feet deep and is thought to be the biggest on Dartmoor. At one point a fence was put around it to stop sheep falling in; the holes for the posts are still there. There are wonderful views from the top of the tor; to the south east you can see Middle Tor and Frenchbeer Rock. Over to the south west you can see the Long Stone ❸, the next stop on the walk.

From Kestor, you head south west along the track towards the Long Stone ❸, which is part of the amazing complex of stone rows and standing stones of Shovel Down, classified as a PAL – or Premier Archaeological Landscape – by Dartmoor National Park. The experts there say: "Shovel Down is the location of a complex of prehistoric ritual monuments, constructed about 4,000 years ago. The presence of five stone rows, a possible stone circle, standing stones and associated burial mounds (cairns) makes this one of the most complex and significant ritual landscapes on Dartmoor."

It is also home to prehistoric field systems, from a slightly later period, about 3,500 years ago. During this time Bronze Age man started dividing up land into fields, and the boundaries are known

INFORMATION

DISTANCE: 5 miles
TIME: 4 hours
MAP: OS Explorer Dartmoor OL28
START POINT: Car park near Batworthy (SX 662 867, TQ13 8EU). On the minor road beyond Teigncombe, two miles west of Chagford
END POINT: Car park near Batworthy
PUBLIC TRANSPORT: Buses from Exeter, Newton Abbot and Okehampton to Chagford. Then taxi to the start.
SWIMMING: Downstream of clapper bridge (SX 655 870) and Tolmen Stone (SX 655 871), North Teign
PLACES OF INTEREST: Kestor Rock, the Long Stone, Scorhill Circle, the Tolmen Stone
REFRESHMENTS: The Courtyard Café, Chagford, an organic wholefood café with great cakes (01647 432571, TQ13 8AE). The Three Crowns Inn, Chagford is an ancient granite thatched building which is worth a visit just to see the historic interior. It serves reasonably priced pub food (01647 433444, TQ13 8AJ).

as reaves. Look out for low, stony, vegetation-covered banks; these are the reaves, and they can be seen mainly in a north east/south west direction. You can also see the remains of the early farmers' round houses, in the form of stone hut circles.

The most prominent of the monuments is the Long Stone. In later times it was adopted as a boundary stone for the three parishes of Chagford, Gidleigh and Lydford (it has the letters C (Chagford), GP (Gidleigh Parish) and DC (Duchy of Cornwall) carved onto it). Think of the outrage there would be today if someone decided to 'graffiti' an ancient monument! There are several double stone rows ❹, which Samuel Rowe, in his 1848 *Perambulation of Dartmoor*, describes memorably as "paral-lelithons". He believes the stone rows were what he calls 'processional roads' of Druidical worship, leading to the Scorhill Stone Circle; there is no real consensus though on what these monuments were for. Other theories are that they were used for worship, or for studying the sun and the moon. Whatever the truth, these historic remains are fascinating.

After exploring the stone relics, it's time to head back northwards and cross the North Teign by the picturesque Teign-e-ver clapper bridge ❺. Although it feels very ancient, and indeed many clapper bridges do go back to medieval times, English Heritage lists it as being probably of 19th century construction. The first swimming spot is a short way downstream from the clapper bridge, by another, much more rudimentary clapper, described by Eric Hemery in *High Dartmoor* (1983) as "badly sited and crudely built", although he describes the area here, between the North Teign and the Wallabrook, as a "wild and beautiful place".

There is a remarkably rectangular channel just below the rudimentary clapper; this is because it is partially man-made, by tinners who walled up the sides to accelerate the current. It's a great little swimming spot; while not the place to do your lengths, it is a fun place to wallow and to play in the waterfalls below. The setting is totally idyllic.

The water then tumbles over a series of cascades, which include the extraordinary Tolmen Stone, a huge boulder with a natural hole in it. Many legends surround this stone, including that if you stand in it you will be cured of whooping cough and rheumatism. There are also claims that the Druids used it for purification and fertility ceremonies.

A little further down is the next pool – broader and rounder than the first, and bordered by rowans. After a refreshing dip, you can walk north for about five minutes to find the Scorhill stone circle ❼, described by Samuel Rowe as "by far the finest example of the rude but venerable shrines of Druidical

worship in Devonshire". It is also one of the best preserved, and least interfered with. Aubrey Burl in his Guide to the Stone Circles of Britain, Ireland and Brittany has a few reservations but is still impressed: "...even with two horrible cart-tracks lurching through it, the ruin retains a bleak grandeur."

As you walk uphill away from the circle, make sure you look back at the view of it, as it is arguably better than when you're up close. The vast, almost barren-looking moor sweeps up behind the circle; if the sun is setting behind the stones the picture is complete. When you reach the crest of the hill, there are more spectacular views, and looking to the right you can see Kestor Rock, where we started.

The walk then takes you off the moor and down a picturesque Devon lane with some beautiful granite cottages. You pass through private woodland, mostly of farmed fir trees, before hearing the enticing sound of the river again, which you cross via a wooden clam bridge. It's a steep climb up the other side before you rejoin the road which takes you back to the starting point.

If you've got the energy after your ascent, it's worth looking at the Bronze Age Round Pound which is just on the right of the road before the parking place. You can clearly see the circle of stones enclosing what would have been the settlement inside. There is evidence that it was used by Iron Age people too. In the 1950s it was excavated and an anvil was found, along with a pair of pits that were used for iron smelting. Later on, in medieval times, it was used again, as some kind of shelter.

DIRECTIONS

1 From the car park, you can see Kestor Rock on the hill to the south; take the path directly to it.
0.3 miles

2 From Kestor, you can see the Long Stone to the south west. Take the path that leads directly from Kestor to the Long Stone.
0.5 miles

3 At the Long Stone, take the path to the right, to the north; you feel as though you're heading back towards the car park.
0.3 miles

4 You reach two double stone rows – follow the path by the left hand stone row. Walk along the path with the wood and stone wall some distance to your right.
0.7 miles

5 You reach the Teign-e-ver clapper bridge. Turn right and walk along with the river on your right. After a few minutes you reach the first swim spot, by a second, very crude, clapper bridge. You are on a little peninsula; to reach the Tolmen Stone and next swim spot, walk on to the end of the peninsula and cross back over, walk a short way downstream and you will find the Tolmen Stone, and just downstream from that, the second swim spot.
0.1 miles

6 Retrace your steps and cross a second clapper bridge over the Wallabrook, and follow the path north east to Scorhill Circle.
0.2 miles

7 After looking at the circle, take the track north east which takes you off the moor via a wooden gate.
0.5 miles

8 Walk down the lane and turn right at the T junction, following the sign for Berrydown and Gidleigh. There is a wooden fingerpost saying Mariners Way, Teigncombe and Road to Kestor Rock.
0.8 miles

9 You will reach a gate on the right which says Gidleigh Wood. Take the track through the gate and into the woods. The path splits; take the right hand fork.
0.4 miles

10 You will start hearing the sound of the river to your left. Ignore the path sign to the right; walk along with the river on your left. Follow the path to the left, following the sign with a yellow arrow that says Path. Cross the clam bridge and follow the path uphill to the right. Keep going uphill, cross a track, and at the top turn right, following the public footpath sign. Then turn left, following the Path sign.
0.5 miles

11 Go through a gate/stile, then turn right into the lane at the top. Follow the lane back to the car park.
0.4 miles

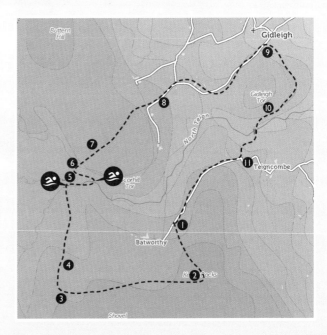

Walk 6

TAVY CLEAVE CIRCULAR

This walk takes you into the famously rugged and mysterious River Tavy valley, home to two of the most magical pools on Dartmoor.

INFORMATION

DISTANCE: 5.5 miles
TIME: 4 hours
MAP: OS Explorer Dartmoor OL28
START POINT: Lane End car park (SX 537 823, PL19 9NB) near Mary Tavy
END POINT: Lane End car park
PUBLIC TRANSPORT: Bus to Mary Tavy: the 46 from Okehampton, Plymouth and Tavistock; the 95 from Horndon and Tavistock; the 188 from Halwill Junction and Tavistock. Then taxi to the starting point.
SWIMMING: Staircase Pool (SX 554 830) and the Devil's Kitchen (SX 555 832): both pools with waterfalls and calm areas
PLACES OF INTEREST: Tavy Cleave Tors, Watern Oke prehistoric village
REFRESHMENTS: The Elephant's Nest Inn in Horndon is the closest pub to the walk. A characterful gastro pub with good ales and wine (01822 810273, PL19 9NQ). The Mary Tavy Inn is cosy with reasonably priced pub food, and nice B&B rooms in a building just by the main pub (01822 810326, PL19 9PN).

This area has been celebrated for its beauty since Victorian times, when Romantic painters such as Frederick Widgery popularised it with artists and a new breed of tourist. While the early part of the walk is easy, the return leg is on unmarked and indistinct paths over open moor, which can be wet and difficult to navigate in mist and cloudy weather, and skirts sheer cliffs. If conditions are difficult then the safer option is to retrace the outward route from Sandy Ford back through the Cleave.

The walk starts by Nattor Farm, built in the 14th century, and which for around two centuries was farmed by the Reep family. They supplied milk to Dartmoor Jail, and in 1939 received an award of £2 for capturing two escaped prisoners. After passing the farm you then follow the Mine Leat, a small man-made waterway which in the 19th century powered seventeen water-wheels servicing three different mines producing tin, copper, lead, silver and even arsenic. It races along, like a sort of water-powered bobsleigh run, and is a fun place to take an inflatable; you can whizz down like a bullet!

Once you reach the head of the Mine Leat, where it siphons off water from the Tavy, you cross it ❷ and start to walk along the river. The river bends around to the left and you are in the Cleave. The Tavy Tors tower over you on the left and the river reveals its secret magic, with two really amazing pools, which must be among the most remote – and dramatic - on Dartmoor. Samuel Rowe, in his *Perambulation of Dartmoor* of 1848, conjures up an evocative picture of a somewhat fairy-tale scene, describing Tavy Cleave as "a magnificent range of castellated tors with which Nature appears to have fortified this fine peninsular hill, while the rapid

stream sweeps round the headland, and forms an effective moat to the titanic citadel above." And he is right. Inside the Cleave, with its plunging cliff sides and its tors up on high, like battlements standing guard, you feel as though you're in a secret, barricaded kingdom of waterfalls, basins, pools and above all, the ever-present sound of rushing water. The river is unusual on Dartmoor in that at many points through the Cleave it runs over a series of flat granite floors, rather than the usual boulders.

The two pools are about three hundred metres apart. The first ❸ has no name, but we've decided to call it 'Staircase Pool' on account of its extraordinary angular waterfalls over a number of granite steps, perfect for playing among the cascades. You can get a really good head and shoulder massage by bracing yourself against the waterfall; you can even get your head behind the thundering water which is quite a surreal experience. The pool below the waterfall is quite shallow so watch out for knocked knees. The second pool is the Devil's Kitchen ❹. No one knows why it's so-called, but it is superb. A seven foot waterfall plunges down into a narrow channel which opens out into a beautiful oval deep pool. The pool is surrounded by huge pink and grey rock platforms, adorned by strange black lichen, like the flock wallpaper you find in an Indian restaurant. Endless fun is to be had in the falls, followed by calm floating in the serene pool. While you are swimming you feel that you are completely in the wild, as far away from the stresses of the 21st century as you could possibly be.

The walk continues up the river. If you are lucky you can see herons, ducks and grey wagtails fishing for brown trout, dabbling for weed or catching mayflies respectively. Small lizards bask on sunny rocks. The walk is now more bouldering than walking, as you continue upstream along the clitter-strewn valley side. Amicombe Brook joins the Tavy at Sandy Ford ❻. You can see the impressive mass of Fur Tor ahead, described by William Crossing as "perhaps the grandest of the Dartmoor tors….a wilderness of stone." There is some disagreement about the name. It is Fur Tor on the Ordnance Survey map, but Eric Hemery, writing in 1983 in *High Dartmoor*, calls it "Vur Tor", because he says this is what the moormen call it. He is scathing about its translation into Fur Tor: "I record my unconditional and deep-felt dislike of this slatternly misuse of traditional Dartmoor place names."

There are some pools you can dip into below Sandy Ford if you're getting hot. The walk then takes in the Watern Oke early Bronze Age settlement. Here there is a group of 90 hut circles in various states of decay. If you look carefully you will be able to make out some in good condition, with their entrances still to be seen. After this you cross Rattle Brook where it is joined by the Dead Lake stream. The crossing point is marked with a boundary stone marked WD 21. WD stands for War Department; it's one of several to mark the Willsworthy firing range. They're thought to date back to about 1900.

The final leg of the walk involves a climb that takes you above the Cleave, and to the Tavy Cleave Tors themselves. The view back down the valley from here is spectacular and well worth the effort. Just be careful, as some of the drops are quite precipitous. As you continue towards the finish you can see Bodmin Moor in the far distance, and Brent Tor, with its distinctive chapel on top, to the south west.

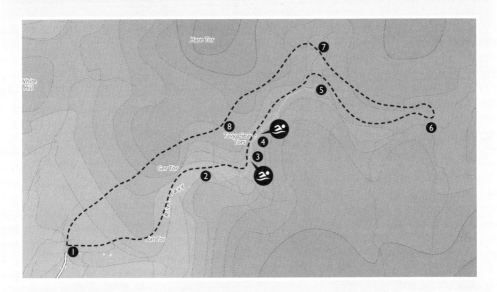

This walk is in the Willsworthy range, so do check firing times before you go on the government website: www.gov.uk/government/publications/dartmoor-firing-programme.

1 From Lane End car park walk directly east along the track to Nattor Farm. From there, follow the Mine Leat on your left, until it reaches the River Tavy – about 25 minutes walk.
1 mile

2 Cross the leat at the concrete bridge, and with the Tavy on your right, follow it upstream. You can walk close to the river in the summer, but in the winter it can be boggy and you may have to walk higher up. After about 15 minutes the river bends round to the left; just round the bend you will see the valley ahead. This is where the Cleave starts.
0.3 miles

3 The first pool we have christened 'Staircase Pool' – this can be found about 10 minutes walk after the bend.
0.1 miles

4 The next pool, the Devil's Kitchen, is another ten minutes' walk.
0.1 miles

5 Carry on up the valley and you will see Rattle Brook entering the Tavy. Ford the river and carry on upstream.
0.4 miles

6 After about 25 minutes you will reach Sandy Ford where the Amicombe Brook joins the Tavy. You then turn to head back and make your way north west over the crest of the hill, to see Watern Oke prehistoric village.
1.2 miles

7 You then need to cross Rattle Brook at Dead Lake Foot, where Dead Lake meets Rattle Brook. It is marked by a boundary stone. Head straight up the other side of the valley and bear south west along an indistinct path around the hillside, above the Cleave, heading for the Tavy Cleave Tors which appear ahead about 20 minutes after leaving Rattle Brook.
1 mile

8 Continue along the indistinct path, following the contours of the hill west towards Ger Tor. From Ger Tor you can then pick up a path downhill back to the car park.
1.2 miles

SANDY HOLE AND EAST DART WATERFALL CIRCULAR

This walk takes you into the remote and sometimes desolate beauty of the High Moor, to a pool cut out of peat, and a spectacular waterfall.

On this walk you'll also see one of the best preserved clapper bridges in the country, and follow an ancient lane once used by the tinners and peat cutters, as well as by folk tending their animals on the moor. If you want, you can also visit the Grey Wethers double stone circle, one of the most spectacular on Dartmoor.

The walk starts in the Postbridge car park ❶, where there's a useful information centre run by the Dartmoor National Park Authority. The village was formed at the end of the 18th century when a new turnpike road was built; its relative modernity is in sharp contrast to the land around it, which was home to Bronze Age people, as evidenced by hut circles and other prehistoric remains.

You follow a path called Drift Lane, part of an ancient north to south route used by people to get to their animals and activities on the moor. As you come through the gate you can see Hartland Tor to your right. The walk then heads uphill. Eric Hemery in *High Dartmoor* describes this part of the moor as 'fen', and it can be very boggy in wet weather. In July 2012 we walked up here, and although it was 'summer' it was tough going and several of us got very wet feet!

After you've crossed Braddon Lake ❸ – which is actually a stream, as on Dartmoor 'lakes' refer to streams – there is interesting evidence of prehistoric man. As you walk up the hill towards the crest of Broad Down, look to your right down towards the river, and take your mind back 3,000 years, when a group of Bronze Age people set up home here. They lived in round houses with thatched roofs, and the hut circles marked on the map as

INFORMATION

DISTANCE: 5.5 miles
TIME: 4-5 hours
MAP: OS Explorer Dartmoor OL28
START POINT: Postbridge car park (SX 646 788, PL20 6SY)
END POINT: Postbridge car park
PUBLIC TRANSPORT: Bus services 23 and 82 from Exeter and Tavistock; the 98 from Yelverton and Tavistock
SWIMMING: Sandy Hole – round pool cut out by peat diggers (SX 624 811); plunge and play at East Dart Waterfall (SX627 810).
PLACES OF INTEREST: Postbridge clapper bridge, Beehive Hut, Roundy Park
REFRESHMENTS: In Postbridge, at the Post Office Stores, they serve hot and cold snacks (01822 880201, PL20 6SY), and the East Dart Hotel, a traditional Dartmoor Inn (01822 880213, PL20 6TJ).

'Broadun Ring' are the remains of their homes. It would have been a good spot, sheltered by Broad Down above and with easy access to the river below.

The top of Broad Down is a plateau, with several outcrops known as the Broadun Rocks ❹. It has breathtaking 360 degree views. If you stand and look back the way you came, you can see, left to right, Hay Tor, Rippon Tor and Buckland Beacon. Walk to the end of the plateau, and looking ahead you can see the East Dart below you, with one of the highest peaks on Dartmoor, Cut Hill, over to the left. In 2010 the BBC reported the discovery of a stone row here; it makes you wonder how many more prehistoric sites have yet to be discovered. The place is certainly remote, and you do get a feeling of isolation which you might find chilling or thrilling. The landscape stretches as far as the eye can see and is featureless and fairly devoid of colour, almost like an old sepia photograph.

Once you get to Sandy Hole ❻, the atmosphere changes, and you can feel the presence of man again. There is a ford, and the pool itself is man-made. People used to cut peat here for fuel, and the sides of the pool are dark and earthy. There

is silky mud underfoot, great to grab in handfuls and spread on the skin, and the mud also means the water heats up much more quickly here than downstream where the water runs over granite. It is a lovely swim, as the pool is fringed with grasses and reeds, and ponies often graze nearby. You can explore upstream (wet shoes are useful), as there is another, shallower pool about 90 metres further on. In the summer when the foxgloves (old Dartmoor name: cowflops) are out, it is idyllic.

In fact this whole area, despite its remoteness, has been the scene of much human activity over the years. It was mined by medieval tinners, who altered Sandy Hole Pass, a small gorge upstream. They deepened it, to create a conduit to take away the water, and there has been some disagreement among the historians as to why. The general consensus though seems to be that it was to speed up the flow of water, and the resulting deposits of sand further downstream gave rise to the name Sandy Hole. This caused problems in Tudor times though, with complaints from Dartmouth, because all the waste sand that washed down the river silted up the harbour.

After a dip and explore at Sandy Hole, the next stop is the East Dart Waterfall ❼, a veritable beauty spot with an unusual curtain of water falling diagonally down a seven foot drop, and then rushing over a series of large ledges to a pool below. William Crossing, in his 1888 guide to walks on Dartmoor, *Amid Devonia's Alps* describes it as a "charming cascade". If there's enough water, you can swoosh down into the pool.

The walk continues by crossing the waterfall (it is best viewed from the northern side), and following the course of the river back to Postbridge. You will notice how the river forms a sharp right angle just after a small island; this is not

natural but was formed by people 'streaming' for tin. The early tin miners would extract tin gravel deposits from the rivers, in a process involving digging trenches so they could 'stream' water over the tin and separate it out from the other minerals. Don't miss the Beehive Hut ❾ a little further on; it looks like an igloo without a roof. Bees were never kept here; it is so-called because of its resemblance to a traditional straw beehive. It was actually built by tinners to store their tools and as a shelter, or perhaps even as a place to stay overnight when out working.

At this point you can do a detour, following the footpath directly north to the stunning Grey Wethers double stone circle. Chris Collier, the author of the respected Stone Circles website (stone-circles.org.uk), has this to say about it: "The question as to why there are two circles here remains unanswered, could the fact that they stand on an almost north-south axis be important, or was it that the two valleys on either side marked an ancient trackway or trade route with each valley belonging to a separate family or tribal group? Did they form the separate meeting place for men and women before some kind of wedding ceremony, perhaps on Sittaford Tor, or were they a place where the recently deceased passed from the land of the living in one circle to the realm of the ancestors in the other? This is a site that poses many more questions than it answers."

Back on the main walk, as you continue along the contours of the hillside you will see a brilliantly well-defined stone wall circle ahead on the other side of the river. This is Roundy Park, the site of a Bronze Age village. The wall would have enclosed their settlement, but has probably been added to over the years by farmers who used it to enclose their livestock. There is a large and well-preserved

kistvaen, or burial tomb there, which was first recorded at the end of the 19th century.

As the walk nears its end you get to Hartland Tor – the only tor on this walk. Apparently there is a hidden memorial to a man from Liverpool, William Donaghy, who died there in a blizzard in 1914. Eric Hemery, in *High Dartmoor*, reports that it is low on the west-south-west slope of the tor, overhung by gorse. We couldn't find it but maybe you can!

When you get back to Postbridge, stop to admire the ancient clapper bridge, thought to have been built in the 13th century. It is one of the finest examples in the country, made of huge slabs of granite, created to enable pack horses carrying tin to cross.

DIRECTIONS

1 Take the path to the left of the Visitor Centre in the car park. Cross the stream, go through the gate and follow the path with the dry stone wall on your right.
0.4 miles

2 The path then heads in a north westerly direction away from the wall; follow it to a little stream called Braddon Lake.
0.4 miles

3 Cross Braddon Lake, go through the stile and walk with the wall on your right. As you go up the hill, the path bends away from the wall towards a stile at the top of the hill. Cross the stile over the stone wall.
0.1 miles

4 Keep walking until you get to a plateau with two rocky outcrops. You will see the East Dart River ahead.
0.5 miles

5 Head west, walking along the contours of the hill; you will see the waterfall below on your right, but don't go there (yet). Keep walking and you will see the rocky gorge of Sandy Hole Pass ahead. The pool is before the pass – you can't miss it, it's big and round.
0.8 miles

6 Swim here, before heading back along the river to the waterfall where you can have another dip.
0.1 miles

7 Cross the waterfall to head back along the northern side of the river.

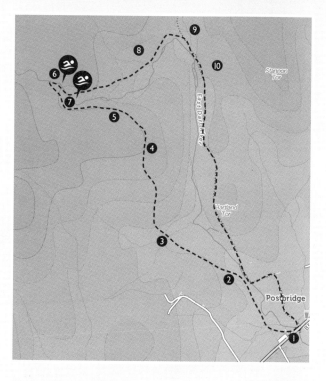

Follow the path above the river, with the river on your right.
0.5 miles

8 You cross a stream – Winney's Down Brook – and pass an island on your right.
0.2 miles

9 Cross another stream, and stop to look at the Beehive hut, about 45 metres to your left after crossing the stream.
0.1 miles (At this point you can do a diversion to visit the Grey Wethers double stone circle. From the Beehive hut, walk a mile north on the bridleway to see the circles, and then retrace your steps to the Beehive.)

10 From the Beehive, follow the path south with the river on your right, past Hartland Tor on your left and down through the wood by the river, and back to Postbridge. **1.7 miles**

67

Walk 8

FOGGINTOR QUARRY AND THE PILA BROOK CIRCULAR

A fascinating adventure through Dartmoor's incredible history and wild nature, taking in a truly unique dip and some breathtakingly beautiful views.

*A*s car parks go, Four Winds is both fascinating and melancholy. Foggintor School once stood here, built straight after the First World War for the children of the quarrymen working at Foggintor, Sweltor and Merrivale. As you can see from the walls that remain around the car park, it was an expansive building with a wood block floor, a leat supplying the water and even central heating – the pipes of which were used to warm the children's pasties. Outside there was a garden with chickens, a goat, rabbits and a beehive. The headmaster to the 55 children was Fred Stoyle, the youngest headmaster in the country.

As the quarries closed and the workers moved away, the school became unviable and it closed in 1936. The building became a private residence renamed Four Winds, although it later fell into disrepair and Dartmoor National Park Planning Authority arranged for it to be demolished in 1964. The headmaster's son Ivan planted the school Christmas tree in the garden in 1924 and you can still see the large evergreen tree growing over the rear wall of the car park.

The walk takes you east out of the car park and up onto Merrivale Down, in the direction of the FM radio and television transmitter at North Hessary Tor. It can be a bit boggy near the leat. You'll soon spot the track leading south to Yellowmeade Farm, but look out for a small hidden pool on the way. This is West Mead Quarry, which was owned and worked by Eric Green and his brother. Eric started working at what was his uncle's quarry aged just 16 and worked for eight hours a day using a 4lb lump hammer. You might also spot

INFORMATION

DISTANCE: 4 miles
TIME: 2-3 hours
MAP: OS Explorer Dartmoor OL28
START POINT: Four Winds Car Park (SX 560 748, PL20 6ST). The car park is two miles west of Princetown on the Tavistock Road (B3357). It's not named, but is the middle of three car parks on this hill and easy to recognise as it has walls and trees round it.
END POINT: Four Winds Car Park
PUBLIC TRANSPORT: The 98 bus service runs between Tavistock and Yelverton (via Princetown) from Monday to Saturday
SWIMMING: Foggintor Quarry (SX 566 736), dipping pools in the Pila Brook at Little Wonder Bridge (SX 548 741)
PLACES OF INTEREST: Four Winds Car Park, Foggintor Quarry, Dartmoor Way, Kings Tor, Merrivale prehistoric monuments
REFRESHMENTS: The Plume of Feathers in Princetown is a great historical inn with slate floors, wooden beams and granite walls, and also offers camping in the field behind, as well as a bunk house (01822 890240, PL20 6QQ). The Dartmoor Inn in Merrivale is a traditional pub run by a local farming family, serving meat reared on Dartmoor and their own farm, and pasties baked in nearby Tavistock (01822 890340, PL20 6ST).

a former explosives store at the quarry before you continue up the hill to the track, over the heather, gorse and fern.

Turning right onto the track, you'll pass Yellowmeade Farm, which is now offering accommodation with stunning moorland views. After the farm you'll spot a metal gate on your right. If you look left from here towards the mast on the hill you'll notice a curious standing stone that doesn't seem entirely natural. If you walk up to it you'll see the letter T carved in one side and an A in the other. This is a TA way marker stone on an old medieval packhorse track. They marked the way between the important stannary towns of Tavistock and Ashburton, the T and the A.

You won't spot Foggin Tor itself, as it no longer exists. It was quarried away, leaving the craggy pit filled with clear water that has long since been reclaimed by nature. As you get closer you will see the remains of Hill Cottages and the manager's house. The quarry ❸ operated for 118 years, employing more than 400 men and supplied granite for London landmarks including Nelson's Column. The granite was also used to build much of Princetown, as well as the huge and imposing Dartmoor Prison.

There are countless myths and legends associated with the moor, and Foggintor Quarry had its own for a while. Between around 1955 and 1980 there were rumours and sightings of eerie humanoid figures lurking in the quarry at night and the locals started to call them the 'Shadow Men'. However, it was later revealed that they had been elite soldiers on top secret training missions. The army still uses the quarry from time to time, while it's also become popular with walkers, climbers and wild swimmers. Not that the latter is anything new. The children of the quarrymen would swim in the quarry pool in the summer and ice skate on it in the winter.

You can enter the quarry and scramble around its left hand walls to reach the deeper water at the far end, or edge around the outskirts and enter from the south. Swim shoes are recommended as there are some sharp submerged rocks, but it's magical once you are in. Swim through the slate-coloured water near the sheer grey cliffs. They rise some 15 meters into the sky, topped with the invading green of the ferns and the gorse with its buttery yellow flowers, the moor restating its claim on this beautiful, plundered valley. It's fun to swim out to the tiny reedy islands or float on your back as the clouds drift past the craggy walls above. If you are braving a bracing winter swim, the moorland mist may just pour over the edge to join you.

Once you've swum and picnicked, climb out of the south of the quarry to walk along what was once a tramway ❹ built in 1823 to allow granite to be taken to Plymouth in horse-drawn trucks. The tramway was rebuilt by the Great Western Railway in 1883 to carry steam engines and coaches out as far as Princetown. It now forms part of the Dartmoor Way, a stunning 95 mile-long circular route through Dartmoor National Park. As you skirt around the imposing King's Tor, look out for the old cutting and sidings of what was once a 'halt' where trains could stop when a flag was raised.

You feel as if you've slightly gone off-piste as you pick your way through boulder-strewn grass. Look out for evidence of quarrying in the form of blocks with holes drilled along their sides, split by feathers and tares. These were metal tools inserted into the holes before being struck with a mallet to cause a break in the granite. As you

go over the stile and head downhill towards the rocks of Hucken Tor and the edge of the trees, don't forget to admire the panoramic view. On a clear day you will see views of Vixen Tor straight ahead, the River Walkham valley to the south, Great Staple Tor to the north and Bodmin Moor on the horizon.

Once you join the bridleway in the woods, you'll cross a lovely stream, the Pila Brook, a tributary of the River Walkham in the valley below. You cross the wonderfully named Little Wonder Bridge ❼, which you can stand underneath, despite it seeming tiny. This has plenty of plunge pools downstream, which can be reached by a short scramble. The bridle path takes you through the grounds of Longash Cottage, which was once a farm. In the days when Foggintor School was open, the head-master's son used to walk here every evening to collect milk for the school children to have at break time the following day. After 10 minutes of being watched by curious black Galloway cattle, you'll come to Hillside Cottage, and back to the main Tavistock Road.

Here there is a chance to paddle in the River Walkham, at the oxbow of the old road where the bridge crosses it. Perhaps more importantly, you can also refresh yourself at the Dartmoor Inn ❽, below the imposing scar of Merrivale Quarry. The 140-year-old pub has a couple of quirky literary connections. Novelist and writer Eden Phillpotts named it The Jolly Huntsman in his novel *The Mother*, with the story set near King's Tor. Meanwhile in *Westward Ho!* Charles Kingsley described it thus:

"On the middle of the down stood a wayside inn; a desolate and lichen-spotted lump of granite, with windows paper-patched and rotting thatch kept down by stones and straw-banks; and at the back a rambling court-ledge of barns and walls, around which pigs and barefoot children grunted in loving communion of dirt."

Today you will be pleased to know it's a really cosy hostelry, renowned for its excellent food.

Merrivale or Tor Quarry was the final Dartmoor quarry to close, in 1997. The New Scotland Yard building is faced with granite from here, while the quarry was also involved in the audacious sale of London Bridge to an American in 1968. When the bridge from the nursery rhyme really was falling down in 1967, a clever PR man in the city of London suggested it could be sold to the Americans as a tourist attraction. Incredibly the ruse worked and an oil entrepreneur purchased it for £1,000,000, although contrary to a popular legend he didn't actually think he was buying Tower Bridge.

The story of American excess continues when the granite blocks, originally mined from Hay Tor quarry, were individually numbered and then transported back from London to Dartmoor and the Merrivale Quarry. Here they were trimmed to size and refinished before being transported by sea to the Port of Houston, Texas and then by rail to the shore of Lake Havasu in Arizona at a further cost of $7 million. However, the businessman wasn't quite the dumb Yank everyone suspected. Property sales at the planned community he had established a few years earlier went through the roof and he easily recouped his outlay with a tidy profit. The bridge became the second most popular tourist attraction in Arizona after the Grand Canyon, while over the past 50 years the population of the city has grown from nothing to 53,000, thanks in no small part to the publicity generated by the incredible story.

After a pub stop, head on back to the car park through Dartmoor's most famous prehistoric monuments, the Merrivale Ceremonial Centre consisting of stone rows, a standing stone, a stone circle and several round stony burial mounds or cairns ❾. Known also as the site of the Potato Market or Plague Market (after a time when food was left here for plague victims), these 4,000-year old arrangements of small and large stones wander monolithically up the hillside in double rows. Interestingly it's been suggested that Dartmoor ponies were used to transport most of the megalithic stones across Britain and, when this system came to an end, they were left to go feral.

The walk through the 4,000-year old ritual complex, up over the wild moorland and back towards the old Fogginitor School car park, perfectly captures what a remarkable place Dartmoor is.

1 Head east uphill from the car park and across the moor towards the television mast at Princetown, keeping parallel to the road until you come to a track leading south to Yellowmeade Farm.
0.3 miles

2 From here it is a level 20 minute walk along a tramway to the unmistakeable ruined buildings and massive granite spoil heaps of Foggintor Quarry. The main water-filled quarry is entered off the track to the left.
0.7 miles

3 At Foggintor, follow the track south out the quarry for a few minutes and then take the second track to the right.
0.2 miles

4 This track is broad and level and was once the Plymouth to Princetown Railway Track before it closed in the 1960s. Now part of the Dartmoor Way, the track heads north west and skirts around King's Tor.
0.9 miles

5 After about 25 minutes the track forks again. Take the right hand, outer track and almost immediately head off the track downhill towards a granite wall with a large timber ladder stile over it. Climb over the stile and head downhill towards the rocks of Hucken Tor and the edge of the trees.
0.4 miles

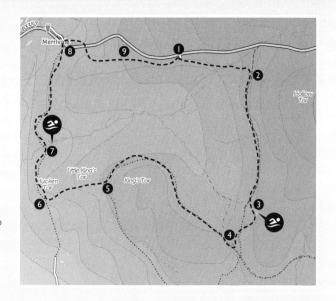

6 After winding your way through outcrops of granite, you will come to a well-defined bridle path in the woods. Turn right onto this (north) and after 15 minutes you will cross a lovely moorland stream, the Pila Brook, a tributary of the River Walkham in the valley below.
0.3 miles

7 Leaving the stream behind, keep following the bridle path to the north through the grounds of Longash Cottage and then Hillside Cottage and back to the main Tavistock Road.
0.6 miles

8 After a possible pub stop at the Dartmoor Inn, head up hill to the east along the main road (B3357) and then branch off to the right as soon as the open moor is reached again.
0.2 miles

9 Follow the wall to the top of the ridge until you see the start of the prehistoric monuments. Once sated with these features, the old Foggintor School car park is just a bit further up the hill.
0.4 miles

THE STEPPING STONES WALK: SHERBERTON, THE WEST DART, THE EAST DART AND HEXWORTHY BRIDGE

This route includes standing stones, mines, open moor and woods, combining peaceful and more popular spots on the West and East Dart Rivers.

*A*s you set off down the lane, enjoying the vistas over open moor out towards Princetown, there is an interesting little detour into Dartmoor's mining history. After 100 metres there is a track leading off to the left, and 50 metres up the track on the right are some well-preserved remains of the 19th century Gobbett tin mine. These include round stones with holes for grinding ore in a crazing mill, and a stone with an indentation, which was a mortar for crushing tin ore.

Back on the main route, you pass Wydemeet on the right, an elegant house which was built in 1914 as a fishing lodge. It later became an adventure centre, and then the home of the famous Polar explorer Pen Hadow. More recently it has been a bed and breakfast, but at the time of writing was up for sale.

As you walk along near Wydemeet you may notice huge tree trunks lying by the road. They're from a sawmill set up by Anton Coaker of Sherberton Farm, which is just nearby. He's a bit of a local celebrity, who has a weekly column in the *Western Morning News*. He's the fifth generation of his family to farm there, and as well as producing sheep and cattle, he's diversified by starting the sawmill and a granite supply operation.

Sherberton Farm is interesting because it's one of the so-called 'ancient tenements' of Dartmoor. These are among the earliest surviving farms on the Moor, established in the 14th century, when certain farmers were allowed to settle and enclose areas of the Forest of Dartmoor. There were seven of these tenements around

INFORMATION

DISTANCE: 7 miles
TIME: 4-5 hours
MAP: OS Explorer Dartmoor OL28
START POINT: Car park (SX650 727, L20 6SD); it's quite remote. From Venford Reservoir, drive north west for about two miles and take the first turning left signposted Sherberton. There is a car parking area shortly along on the right just before the cattle grid.
END POINT: Car park
PUBLIC TRANSPORT: None
SWIMMING: Swincombe Meet (SX 647 737), East Dart (SX 671 742), Hexworthy Bridge (SX 658 729)
PLACES OF INTEREST: Dunnabridge Pound, Laughter Man Standing Stone, Dartmeet, St Raphael's Church

REFRESHMENTS: Badger's Holt, Dartmeet, a former fishing lodge with tables outside along the river bank, specialising in cream teas (01364 631213, PL20 6SG). Brimpts Farm, Dartmeet has a tearoom, bunkhouse and camping (0845 0345968, PL20 6SG)

Wellies or good waterproof boots are advisable for this walk. The route includes three sets of stepping stones which may be covered after heavy rain, and some boggy areas of moor alongside the Swincombe.

the West Dart, including Sherberton. In return for their right to enclose and graze their animals, the farmers had various duties including rounding up stray cattle and ponies (the 'drifts') and impounding them at Dunnabridge Pound, which we will see later on the walk. If you want to look at the farm you can do a short detour up the road just by the first set of stepping stones.

This first set of stones – across the River Swincombe ❷ - is a bit of a warm-up to the next set, which is a lot bigger. Stepping stones tend to be referred to simply as 'steps' on Dartmoor. They're great fun, but can be tricky to cross, especially if they're wet and you don't have a great sense of balance. So take care and if in doubt, wade! You don't want a broken ankle at this stage of the game.

Thread your way through a boggy area, following the river downstream, and after 10 minutes you will reach a sedate bend in the West Dart where the Swincombe joins it. This is known as Swincombe Meet ❸. Framed by pine trees this is a beautiful place for a picnic and, of course, a swim. We call it the 'Winnie the Pooh place' on account of the pine trees. It's easiest to cross the stepping stones and swim from the other side where there is a 'beach'. In the spring the hillsides around are carpeted with bluebells and it could not be more idyllic. It's fun to snorkel too and spot numerous trout, and if you've got small children they can have fun fishing for minnows in the shallows.

The walk continues with the West Dart on your left, before you reach the main road where you will see the magnificent Dunnabridge Pound ❹, which is thought to date back to the Bronze Age. In medieval times it was used to impound animals, which were rounded up during the drifts. The most noteworthy and intriguing thing about it is a granite 'seat' that looks as though it was made from some

of the smaller bits of Stonehenge. It's known as the Judge's Chair, and old Dartmoor legend has it that it came from the Stannary Parliament at Crockern Tor, over to the west. This idea seems to have been largely discredited but it does seem likely that, as William Crossing suggests in his *Guide to Dartmoor*, some enterprising farmer in the past used ancient dolmens found on the moor to construct a shelter for those who were looking after the animals in the pound. Further on in the walk we will see a standing stone and a stone row, so it seems eminently possible that these could have been used. You can just imagine the farmers of the past sheltering in the chair from the unforgiving Dartmoor weather.

From the pound, you head onto the open moor, following the stone track. There are great views; to the west is Crockern Tor, the meeting place of the Stannary Parliament, and the impressive Longaford and High White Tors to the north. Cresting the hill, Bellever Tor also appears. After passing through a second gate, note the impressive standing stone to your left below Laughter Tor. This is known as the Laughter Man, or originally, the Lough Tor Maen. There is also an incomplete stone row of at least five stones, which is very well camouflaged among the gorse and marram grass, but is satisfying to find.

The walk then takes you through coniferous forest, which was planted in the 1920s by the Duchy of Cornwall. Opinions vary as to whether this was a good thing. You wind down through the woods, going past elegant Laughter Hole House, with its beautiful manicured gardens, a contrast to the wilderness that surrounds it. Back in 2003 an estate agent was fined for describing it as a property with a royal connection, claiming it had once been King Edward VIII's hunting lodge. In fact, it was built in 1912 for Raleigh Phillpotts, who was a distant relation of the author Eden Phillpotts, who wrote many novels about Dartmoor.

You then cross the third set of stepping stones ❻ of the walk, before heading up and through Babeny Farm. This is another of the ancient tenements, like Sherberton at the beginning of the walk, and is currently occupied by the fourth generation of Wilkinsons, who operate it as a successful riding stables.

The walk then takes you down the East Dart to Dartmeet ❾. There are several swimming spots, but the best can be found where the valley opens out, the river slows and there are large grassy areas ❽. Nowhere is particularly deep, so it's more fun for plunging and playing, but nevertheless it is an idyllic place to stop. As you near Dartmeet it gets busier, particularly at the weekends and during the holidays. There is an ice cream shop and the Badger's Holt restaurant which serves meals or cream teas in high season. Dartmeet is one of those 'honeypot' spots where the majority of people seem happy to sit by their cars. It also has the remains of a once-spectacular clapper bridge.

Moving on from Dartmeet, you reach the very special St Raphael's Church ❿, which is usually open. It is particularly beautiful in spring, when it is surrounded by snowdrops. Inside, it is austere but stunning, and, unusually, has a wood burning stove. It was built in 1869 as a mission chapel for those who lived too far away from the main parish church at Lydford. It was designed to be both a place of worship and a school; the wooden desks are still in place today, and used as pews.

Shortly after the church you will come to another swimming spot, at Hexworthy Bridge which was sketched by JMW Turner when he visited Dartmoor. The river bends beautifully here, and

you can have a lovely swim, especially in the deeper part on the outside of the bend. You may well have spectators, as this is another honeypot where people like to park their cars and have a picnic.

After a refreshing dip, it's a short walk back to where you started.

DIRECTIONS

❶ From the car park, cross the cattle grid and head west down the lane. You reach a bridge over the River Swincombe. Cross it, and turn right onto a public bridleway, and then cross back over the Swincombe via the first set of stepping stones.
0.6 miles

❷ Walk with the river on your left, until you reach the second set of stepping stones.
0.3 miles

❸ Cross over. This is the first swimming spot, Swincombe Meet. After your swim, walk on with the river on your left, and then bear right, following the path uphill to the road.
0.6 miles

❹ At the road turn left and cross the cattle bridge. Stop to admire Dunnabridge Pound. Follow the outside wall of the pound to the west and pass through a gate onto the open moor. Take the

well-defined stone track ahead of you which bears right gently uphill, signposted Public Bridlepath Laughter Hole Farm. Follow the path all the way to the pine forest.
0.9 miles

❺ Go through the gate and take the track which forks to the right downhill. At the bottom by the house on the left, turn right, almost back on yourself, following the sign that says Public Bridlepath

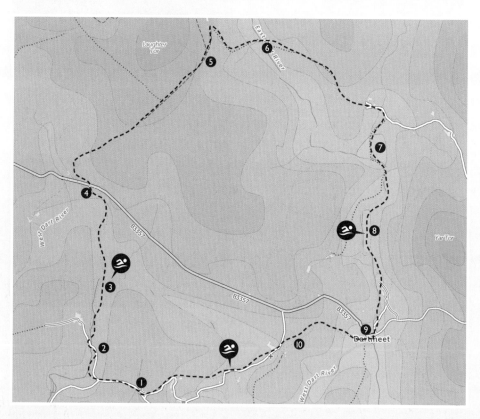

to Sherrill via Babeny. Do not follow the track to the right. Follow the path downhill, through a five-bar gate, and over a footbridge, until you reach a set of stepping stones over the East Dart.
0.5 miles

6 Follow the path up the side of the hill, pass through a gate onto a well signposted bridle path and after 20 minutes you will walk through Babeny Farm.
0.7 miles

7 Pass over a bridge which spans a lovely rocky cascade and after a few minutes, when you reach a car turning space, cross over a small steam and follow it downhill to re-join the East Dart.
0.4 miles

8 Follow the East Dart downstream (with the river on your right) towards Dartmeet. The best swimming spot is where there is a large grass clearing.
I mile

9 At Dartmeet, cross the bridge to an old garage on the left and follow the Huccaby path between the buildings and through a gate. Then follow the path right uphill until you come to another gate and keep right again, into a rock-walled track. At the top of the hill cross the field to the barns of Huccaby Farm. Keep right on the track and then turn left onto the road. Ahead is the small but perfectly formed church of St Raphael.
0.6 miles

10 Keep on the road and you will shortly arrive at Hexworthy Bridge, another lovely swimming spot. After the bridge, turn right immediately over a stone stile. Head over green fields and stone stiles until you come to the tiny hamlet of Hexworthy. Take the track to the right, between the thatched cottages, and follow this uphill for 10 minutes. At the top bear right and you will be back at the car park.
I mile

79

Walk 10

CRAZYWELL CIRCULAR

This is a spectacular walk, with majestic views of tors and the sea that make you feel as though you are literally on top of the world.

At the start of the walk, as you ascend, you see the grey mass of Down Tor to your right. Don't forget to look behind you every so often for increasingly impressive views of the shiny mirror of Burrator Reservoir spread out below, with Sheeps Tor looming behind it. Just before you turn off the path to get to Crazywell Pool, you will see Crazywell Cross ahead on the brow of the hill. It's believed to be one of several old crosses on the moor which marked a track followed by monks travelling between Buckfast and Tavistock Abbeys. It's one of many ancient crosses which Dartmoor National Park has now microchipped, in order to deter thieves. The plundering of these ancient artefacts has been a real problem in the past.

When you get to Crazywell Pool ❸ - which is shaped like an enormous lozenge - it feels rather surreal, almost as though one has stepped into an alien world. The Victorian writer Eden Phillpotts incorporated it into the plot of one of his novels: "Like a cup lies Crazywell upon the waste… a haunt of mystery and a water of power". It has a vast, open feel and one friend describes it as a 'lido on the moor'. The pool is rumoured to be bottomless, probably because its waters are so dark and mysterious, but it's actually only about four metres deep, and is probably the result of tin mining. It has some wonderful legends: that the water level rises and falls with the tides down at Plymouth Sound; that on some nights a voice is heard, announcing the name of the next person from the parish to die; and that on Midsummer's Eve, if you look into the pool, you will see the face of the next person to die. No one knows how it got its outlandish name. In the first OS map of 1809 it appears as Classenwell Pool; other names over the years include Clacywell, Classiwell and

INFORMATION

DISTANCE: 4 miles
TIME: 4 hours
MAP: OS Explorer Dartmoor OL28
START POINT: Norsworthy Bridge north of Burrator Reservoir (SX 567 693, PL20 6PE)
END POINT: Norsworthy Bridge
PUBLIC TRANSPORT: Only on Sundays: the 48 bus from Plymouth
SWIMMING: Crazywell Pool – a large lake high up on the moor (SX 582 704) and Hart Tor Waterfall (SX 575 715)
PLACES OF INTEREST: Crazywell Cross, Crazywell Pool, Hart Tor Stone Rows
REFRESHMENTS: There are none on the walk, so it's a good idea to bring a picnic. Nearby in Princetown is the Plume of Feathers pub, where you can also camp or stay in their bunkhouse (01822 890240, PL20 6QQ). Another excellent option is the Fox Tor café in Princetown, legendary for its cake and friendly welcome, which also has a bunkhouse, and you can hire bikes (01822 890238, PL20 6QS).

Clazywell. It is an absolutely magical place to swim. The water is clean, the pool is huge, and the sense of isolation is breathtaking. In this vast spread of water, you can laze as the larks sing overhead, or else put your head down and do some serious lengths.

After your dip, as you head north you'll get to Devonport Leat, which was built in the 1790s to take water down to the docks at Devonport in Plymouth. It's a great example of human ingenuity, channelling water by using gravity to divert it from the freshwater rivers on the high moor, and taking it down to the settlement where it was needed. Just before the leat starts to drop downhill, you can see the clear outlines of the Raddick Hill prehistoric huts enclosed by a perimeter wall, just down the slope to the left. There are two really clear hut circles right by the leat, and it is easy to imagine the Bronze Age village of small thatched huts surrounded by its protective wall.

As you start to descend down the leat, note the distinctive tor on the valley side opposite. It's Black Tor, though we've rechristened it 'Barbara Hepworth Tor' as the stones are reminiscent of her famous sculptures. There is a logan stone on top, which can be rocked. There are various logan stones on Dartmoor, which are naturally occurring due to weathering in the rock. There are various legends around them, including that the Druids used them in their worship.

The next stop on the walk is a charming small waterfall on the Hart Tor Brook ❺. It's a perfect place for a picnic and a plunge. Surrounded by small trees, and in a little hollow, it feels like an enchanted spot. Five minutes further uphill, and across the Brook, there are the Hart Tor stone rows and circles ❻, a good example of a Bronze Age monument. There are two stone rows, one double and one single, each with a circle at the end containing a cairn. The rows were first mentioned by Samuel Rowe in his *Perambulation of Dartmoor* in 1848, where he describes them as a

"pair of avenues...about two and a half feet high", and observes: "It is somewhat remarkable that these avenues have escaped entire demolition, as they are intersected diagonally by an old stream work." The stream work he mentions refers to tin mining, which undoubtedly led to the destruction of parts of this ancient monument. It is still quite shocking today to see how those tin miners were quite happy to drive their course right through the middle of the stone row. Nevertheless, it is much visited, and has been much discussed in archaeological literature, although no one really knows why our forefathers built these fascinating stone rows.

After exploring the rows, you head back to the leat passing the aqueduct which is known locally as the Iron Bridge. Follow it down through the plantation and past ruined Leather Tor Farm **8**. The farm – which dates back to the medieval period - was abandoned in the 1920s because it was in the catchment area for the then new Burrator Reservoir, and the owners did not want any farming in the area. It's a reminder of just how much influence man has had on Dartmoor; we tend to think of it as a wild, untamed place, but creations like the reservoirs have had a major effect on the landscape.

Just after the farm, as you turn left and start walking downhill towards the bridge, look out for a cave on the left that looks rather like a Hobbit hole. The cavern extends back over thirty feet, and may originally have been dug by tinners to store their tools. More recently it was used by the occupants of Leather Tor Farm to store potatoes.

The final water crossing of the walk is over Leather Tor Bridge, the last clapper bridge to be built on Dartmoor, in 1833. There has been a crossing here since Bronze Age times, when there was (and still is) a ford and stepping stones, a few of which are still in the river.

DIRECTIONS

1 Take the well-defined track uphill to the north east from Norsworthy Bridge and keep bearing right at the first and second forks in the track. After about 20 minutes you leave the forest behind and the track continues onto the open moor. After another 5 to 10 minutes, you will see a stone cross – Crazywell Cross - on the ridge in front of you.
1.2 miles

2 Then you will see a very large ditch to your left, with a stream running through it and across the path. Turn immediately left here and follow the ditch uphill to Crazywell Pool.
0.1 miles

3 After a cold swim, head north up hill and you will hit Devonport Leat. Cross the leat (there are several small bridges) and follow it to the west, eventually dropping sharply down the hillside.
0.8 miles

4 Halfway down the hill, take an indistinct path to the right, walking north with the River Meavy in the valley below to your left.
0.1 miles

5 After about 10 minutes you will reach the Hart Tor Brook Waterfall. Cross the brook via the top of the waterfall, or a little metal bridge slightly further up, and head north for about 180 metres until you reach the stone rows.
0.1 miles

6 From the stone rows, head south by the Meavy until you pass the aqueduct on your left, and follow the leat all the way to the plantation.
0.6 miles

7 At a gate, join the forest track signposted Crossgate and Yennadon which continues to follow the leat. After about five minutes, take the path branching off to the left downhill, signposted Leather Tor Farm.
0.7 miles

8 At the farm, go through the gate ahead and turn left down the track, signposted Older Bridge. In fact the first bridge you come to is Leather Tor Bridge. Cross the bridge and then turn right, signposted Norsworthy Bridge.
0.1 miles

9 Follow the track as it runs parallel to the River Meavy down-stream. Re-join the track you set out on at the start and turn right to come back to the car park.
0.4 miles

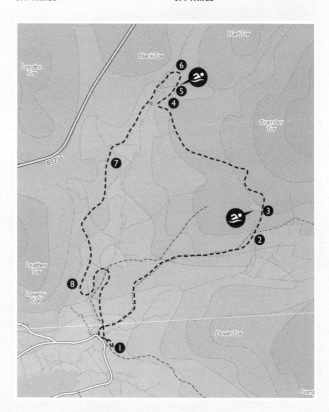

Walk 11

SHARRAH POOL CIRCULAR

Experience the raw purity of the River Dart rushing through a wooded gorge, a steep ascent to a remarkable tor, and a picturesque Dartmoor village.

INFORMATION

DISTANCE: 5 miles
TIME: 3 hours
MAP: OS Explorer Dartmoor OL28
START POINT: Newbridge (SX711 708, TQ13 7NT). Park in the small car park by the road on the Ashburton side of the bridge
END POINT: Newbridge
PUBLIC TRANSPORT: Buses: the X38 from Exeter and Plymouth, and the 88 from Newton Abbot and Totnes. Then you'll need to taxi to the start point
SWIMMING: Sharrah Pool (SX 697 716) on the River Dart, plus numerous smaller pools
PLACES OF INTEREST: Sharrah Pool, Bench Tor, Holne Parish Church (which is notable for its rare medieval painted roodscreen)
REFRESHMENTS: The Holne Tea Rooms, a wonderful village enterprise, with excellent food and friendly villagers serving it (01364 631188, TQ13 7SL). The Church House Inn at Holne, a traditional country pub (01364 631208, TQ13 7SJ)

You start in ancient woodland, walking past a whole series of cascades, chutes and pools, many of which are suitable for swimming in. This is one of the most beautiful stretches of the River Dart. The water is invariably clear, passing as it does over pure granite. You can normally see trout, as well as minnows and bullheads in the shallows. The woods are gorgeous at all times of the year, whether in the starkness of winter, in the acid green growth of spring, or in the autumn, when fungi, including penny buns, chanterelles and hedgehog mushrooms can be found. After about a quarter of an hour's walk you climb a steep hill to the top of Holne Cliff, from where you can see down to a big pool below. This is known locally as Betsy's Pool, and is off Wellsfoot Island, which has a sandy beach. There are also amazing views up the Dart Gorge from the top of Holne Cliff.

You go down the other side of the hill and keep walking until you reach a spectacular waterfall ❸, which you need to cross. You are now walking high above the river, and down below are various islands. Eventually you reach a stile, and a few minutes further on you reach Sharrah Pool ❹. It is unmistakeable, because it's absolutely huge. It has a most magical waterfall at the top, with enormous rocks, one of which has been christened Elephant Rock by outdoor swimmers. The thing to do is the 'Sharrah Chute', which involves climbing onto Elephant Rock, and then jumping out into the current and getting swept down like a cork popping out of a champagne bottle. Just down from the cascade, you zoom through a rectangular channel, with 'walls' of granite, before the pool opens out into a vast oval. Once floating in the pool, if you look upstream and then up, you will see the rocky buttress of Bench Tor, overlook-

ing the pool like a castle standing sentinel. It's not known how the pool got its name. Some think it may be a corruption of 'Sarah's Pool', but as to who Sarah was, nobody knows.

Once you've enjoyed a swim, the walk then takes you on a virtually vertical climb, about five hundred feet up to Bench Tor. You'll get so hot climbing up through the woods you'll probably want another swim, which is possible towards the end of the walk. Once you get to Bench Tor **❼** the views down over the Dart Gorge are absolutely magnificent. You can hear the rush of the river, as well as see it, and you can even make out Sharrah Pool down below. Eric Hemery, in *High Dartmoor*, says the Tor was described as 'Benjay Tor' in the first edition of the OS one inch map in 1809, and he calls it 'Benjy Tor. However, Bench Tor would seem a suitable name, as unlike most Dartmoor tors it is much wider than it is high. It spreads in groups of rock along a promontory, and according to Hemery, one of the outcrops was once known as 'Eagle Rock', probably because of the habitat's wild, isolated suitability for the bird, before it disappeared and fled to Scotland.

Once you've explored all around the tor, and taken in its tremendous views, you then walk south and pick up the road to Holne **❽**. This is a beautiful Dartmoor village, with a particularly good tea shop, run by volunteers. They certainly don't stint on the cream in their cream teas! Or if that doesn't take your fancy you can have a refreshing pint in the pub.

After a pit stop, it's pretty much downhill all the way back. You head along the footpath down through a couple of fields and then pick up the path by the river, just near where you started. There are several pools along here if you fancy another dip before going home.

DIRECTIONS

1 Walk along the eastern/southern bank of the Dart, keeping the river on your right.
0.1 miles

2 After about five minutes you will reach a fork – with a signpost to Holne pointing to the left hand fork. Ignore this and stay on the path going alongside the river.
0.3 miles

3 After about 35 minutes walk – in which you ascend a big hill and go down again - you cross a waterfall.
1 mile

4 After another 10–15 minutes walk you will reach a stile. Head over and down the path where you will see Sharrah Pool up ahead on the right.
0.5 miles

5 After a swim, come back to the stile and turn immediately right and follow the fence right up through the woods - a very steep climb. Follow the path until it comes out of the woods, and along to a field gate.
0.3 miles

6 At the gate turn right and follow the field boundary on your left, and then bear right to Bench Tor which you will see up ahead.
0.3 miles

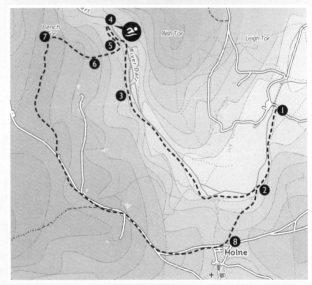

7 Once you've explored Bench Tor, turn back and follow the stone wall on your left. It will take you to the road, where you turn left and walk down into the village of Holne.
2 miles

8 Once you've explored Holne, re-join the road where you will find a fingerpost sign to a path which leads you down through fields and back to the river.
0.3 miles

9 The path links up with the very first section of path; follow it back up to your car.
0.4 miles

Walk 12

WARHORSE POOL AND SHAVERCOMBE WATERFALL CIRCULAR

Take in one of the most spectacular prehistoric sites on Dartmoor, a hidden waterfall and a farm which was the location for a Hollywood film.

INFORMATION

This walk involves crossing a river, so it's best done in dry sunny weather, when the water is low. This allows you to see the monuments to their best advantage too.

DISTANCE: 5 miles
TIME: 4 hours
MAP: OS Explorer Dartmoor OL28
START POINT: Scout Hut car park (SX 578 673, PL20 6PG), east of the village of Sheepstor
END POINT: Scout Hut car park
PUBLIC TRANSPORT: Sunday bus 48 from Plymouth to Burrator Reservoir; then walk from the village of Sheepstor to the start at the Scout Hut
SWIMMING: Warhorse Pool, River Plym (SX 587 662) and Shavercombe Waterfall (SX 594 660)
PLACES OF INTEREST: Drizzlecombe Stone Rows, Giant's Basin, Eylesbarrow Tin Mine
REFRESHMENTS: The Burrator Inn, Dousland, known as the 'Burrie', serving reasonably priced pub grub (01822 853121, PL20 6NP). The Royal Oak, Meavy, is an award-winning pub in a picturesque location on the village green (01822 852944, PL20 6PJ)

The walk starts off along a track heading towards the north east, and looking ahead you get a glimpse of Higher Hartor Tor up on the right. Back down to the left, you can see the mountainous mass of Sheeps Tor, which has had many names over the years, with the first name – Sitelestorra – recorded in 1168. Back in 1474 it was known as Shittestor, but the rather more palatable name of Sheeps Tor is now in use.

Along the track to the left you will notice marker stones, bearing the inscription 'PCWW 1917' ❷. These were erected by the Plymouth Corporation Water Works to mark the boundary of Burrator Reservoir. Further along you come to the fascinating remains of the Eylesbarrow tin mine which was worked in the early 19th century. To the right of the track you'll see a large piece of wall with a hole in it to the right. This was stamping mill number two, where the mined ore was finely crushed so it could be separated from the waste. The hole is where the axle went. Most of the mine though is on the left hand side of the track.

The existence of the mine was first recorded in 1804 when shares were advertised for sale. Be careful as you explore, as many of the shaft heads are still there, in conical pits. There is what looks like the remains of a large rectangular building. This was the wheel pit, built in 1815 to house the waterwheel. You will also see what looks like a double stone row. This is not in fact a prehistoric feature, but another remnant of the old mine. It's the remains of a so-called 'flatrod' system of linked iron or wooden rods, which linked the waterwheel to

the mine shafts. As the waterwheel turned it pushed the flatrods, which in turn powered the underground pumps at the mineshafts further up the hill. It must have been pretty bleak being a tin miner out working in the wilds of Dartmoor, with very few creature comforts.

The walk then takes you down the Drizzlecombe Valley with a stream running through. Here you will pass the remains of more buildings, and after you cross the stream and ascend to the brow of the hill you will find yourself among one of the most extensive Bronze Age settlements on the moor. A series of hut circles ❺ look down on three stone rows ❻. Hansford Worth, author of one of the most famous and authoritative guides to Dartmoor, describes them as "the most neatly arranged group on Dartmoor, and, with the possible exception of Merrivale, the sole example which shows what by our modern standards would be regarded as planning." He was the first to write about them, and when he first observed them the terminal stones, or menhirs, were lying flat on the ground. They were re-erected in 1893. They are truly breathtaking, and contain what is said to be the tallest terminal stone on Dartmoor, known as the 'Bone Stone', which is over four metres high. These mysterious megaliths set the mind wondering about our ancestors. The truth is, although there are many theories about why these rows were built, no one really knows what they were for, or how they were used.

Looking southwards along the rows, you will see an enormous cairn which is known as the Giant's Basin. It's hollowed out at the top, probably where treasure seekers explored in the past, or where local farmers took the stones. Some important tribal leader is buried here, but whether or not the cairn dates from the same

time as the stone rows is not known.

The walk then takes you up the Shavercombe stream; a tiny, trickling watercourse. The waterfall ❼ comes as a delightful surprise, as there is no sign of it until you are right there. As Eric Hemery puts it in *High Dartmoor*, "the stream, in its upper reach, is comparatively featureless…But the metamorphosis is to come: abruptly the granite ceases, and the brook falls headlong into a deep, dark canyon of eroded sedimentary rock, quite hidden…". It feels like a secret room with bright-green moss-lined walls; the waterfall thunders down a vertical drop, and as you sit in the bowl of water below you feel as though you're in an enchanted bower. The waterfall is surrounded by rowans, oaks and sycamore and is truly memorable. It's a place to wallow and feel immersed in the secret beauty of Dartmoor.

The main swimming spot is in a weir pool ❽, not far away, down below in the River Plym. The weir was created to siphon off water for a leat

which was needed to power a nearby tin mine. The water is an amazing golden colour; it is calm and deep, and is the perfect place for a refreshing dip. It's beautifully clear and gets the sun all day.

After your dip, the walk takes you past Ditsworthy Warren Farm, a fascinating old building which featured in the Steven Spielberg film, *Warhorse*, as Narracott Farm. It must be one of the remotest farmsteads on the moor, and is now semi-derelict and rather gloomy; Spielberg gave it a thatched roof to pretty it up for the movie. In its heyday in Victorian times, and in the first half of the 20th century, the farm was the breeding place of thousands of rabbits, bred for both their meat and their fur. It had various warreners, including one, Nicholas Ware, who had a wooden leg. He can't have found it easy, given the terrain. The final warrener was a formidable matriarch known as Granny Ware, who ruled the place with a rod of iron and who died in 1945. The farm is now owned by the army who occasionally use it for military exercises.

From the farm, as you walk back along the track, you see the fairly new rubble surface underfoot, put there to enable the film crews to get all their equipment up to the farm. This walk really does illustrate the hugely different ways in which man has used the moor over thousands of years. From the Bronze Age people, through to the tin miners, warreners and film makers, as Eric Hemery puts it, "the pageant of human endeavour on Dartmoor is here in a perfect setting".

DIRECTIONS

1 From the car park, walk past the scout hut on your right and take the track in a north easterly direction. After about 20 minutes you pass a boundary stone on your left, and then another. Both read 'PCWW 1917'.
0.5 miles

2 From the boundary stones, keep going for about another 20 minutes you reach a path on the right.
0.4 miles

3 At this junction, keep on going for a short detour of about ten minutes to see the remains of the Eylesbarrow Tin Mine. Afterwards retrace your steps to the junction
0.7 miles there and back to point 3.

4 Once back at the junction, follow the path south (to the left) and you will come across more ruins on your left. Just after three distinctive large pillars, turn left and walk down into the little valley. Cross the Drizzlecombe Brook and head up the other side.
0.3 miles

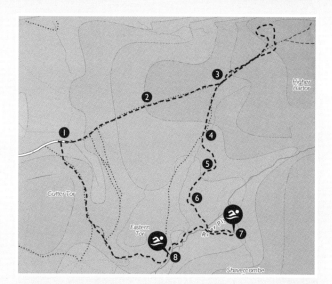

5 At the crest of the hill turn right, and you will arrive at numerous hut circles and then the Drizzlecombe Stone Rows.
0.3 miles

6 At the bottom standing stone turn left, and head for the river. Cross the river at the ford, and follow the path for a short time, with Shavercombe Brook on your

right, before turning right and crossing the stream via a small ford. Follow the path beside the stream (the stream is now on your left) until you reach the waterfall.
0.6 miles

7 From the waterfall, retrace your steps back down to the main river Plym. Walk south

beside the river until you reach Warhorse Pool – you can't miss it, as there is a weir.
0.7 miles

8 At Warhorse Pool, it's easiest to swim from the other side. After your swim, follow the path up the hill towards Ditsworthy Warren Farm. Pick up the track by the house and follow it back to the car park.

Walk 13

CENTRAL DARTMOOR LAKES

This walk takes you right into the heart of Dartmoor, to these lonely lakes in their forlorn grandeur, watery remnants of a once-active mining industry on the moor.

INFORMATION

DISTANCE: 12 miles there and back
TIME: 6-7 hours
MAP: OS Explorer Dartmoor OL28
START POINT: Harford Gate car park near Ivybridge (SX 643 595, PL21 0JQ)
END POINT: Harford Gate car park
PUBLIC TRANSPORT: None to Harford Gate, but buses and trains at Ivybridge, from both Plymouth and Exeter. From the town it is a 2.6 mile walk along the Two Moors Trail which links up to the Puffing Billy Track
SWIMMING: Leftlake (SX 647 634), Red Lake (SX 645 669)
PLACES OF INTEREST: Eastern White Barrow, mine remains at Red Lake
REFRESHMENTS: Pubs and cafés in Ivybridge, including the Riverbank Café with great views over the River Erme (01752 698576, PL21 9PS). Also the Cornwood Inn, in the nearby village of Cornwood, is a friendly Dartmoor pub serving a good range of reasonably priced food (01752 837225, PL21 9PU).

We think of this walk as the 'Long March'. It's an effort to get to the lakes, but it's worth it, because swimming here is an otherworldly experience, like being on some faraway planet. It's a whole day trip, but it also makes a great adventure to camp overnight at Red Lake. Keep equipment to a minimum though as you have to carry it a long way!

For by far the greater part of this walk you will be on the Two Moors Way, which in this part of Dartmoor follows the track of an old tramway which carried miners to the china clay works at Red Lake. Mining began here in 1910, when the railway track was created. The path is known locally as the Puffing Billy track, as small steam engines travelled along it, carrying workers and equipment up to the mine in little carriages.

It's strange to imagine the trains busily steaming up and down this track, carrying miners who no doubt lived and worked in pretty dire conditions. Dartmoor has been exploited by man in many different ways throughout the ages for many commodities, including tin, peat and water. Indeed china clay mining is still going on today at nearby Lee Moor, and a new tungsten mine has just opened at Hemerdon. For most of us now Dartmoor is a place of recreation, a place to visit, and a place to find beauty and solace from our busy lives. But in the past it was a place of industry, where people lived, worked and battled to survive.

As you walk, enjoy the feeling of isolation as you get further and further away from civilisation. On sunny summer days the larks sing overhead, and you can see for miles across the vast

open scenery. Look out for Piles Copse, down the valley to the west of you, one of Dartmoor's three ancient woodlands, with twisted stunted oaks and mossy boulders. There is a wonderful little stream and waterfall there too. Beyond that you can see Stalldown Barrow; you might even be able to make out its famous stone row on top of the ridge, and further on Erme stone row – one of the longest stone rows in Europe. An alternative circuit, which loops back via these sites in the Erme valley, is briefly described in the directions.

The environment starts to become almost featureless as you make your way towards the moor's interior, but that is one of the most beautiful aspects of this walk. You can almost lose yourself in the enormity of the landscape, its muted colours, and the vast sky. You can get into a good rhythm walking along the track, and it can be a meditative experience. When you reach the first swimming spot, Leftlake ❷, the water greets you like an oasis, a vast shiny pool, and it's impossible not to want to jump in.

On Dartmoor, 'lake' usually refers to a stream, rather than a large area of water. Indeed you will see small streams on the OS map marked as 'lakes'. The author Eric Hemery, in *High Dartmoor*, says he believes the use of the word indicates the fact that the source of the streams was often a lake or tarn. For convenience, we refer to the actual lakes in this chapter as 'Red Lake' and 'Leftlake' as well, which we hope is not too confusing!

There is a bridge over Leftlake - again, a remnant of the old railway, which is pretty well preserved. Swimming in the lake is intensely pleasurable. The water is the colour of dark amber, and moving through it, your limbs look as though they've had rather an overenthusiastic dose of spray tan. You can float on your back, listening to the larks above, drifting in the enormous pool. There's plenty of room for practising your strokes, or why not organise some swimming races? Anything is possible!

After your dip at Leftlake, you continue along the Two Moors Way, deeper into the heart of the moor, towards Red Lake. Look out for the spectacular Bronze Age cairn, Eastern White Barrow, a mile to your right, known locally as the 'Dartmoor Submarine' because of its unusual shape. William Crossing describes it (in his *Guide to Dartmoor*) as "a very fine example of an ancient burial heap". The Bronze Age person who was buried here must have been pretty important. The cairn has an unusual stone tower on top, which gives it the appearance of a submarine. It is thought the tower was a later addition but no one really knows who added it or why.

The final approach to Red Lake ❹ is tantalising, because the path is sunk between two banks.

You know you're getting nearer, because you can see a large cone-shaped hill up ahead – the spoil heap from the china clay workings. However you don't get to see the water until you're right there. The first thing to do is climb to the top of the conical hill, a.k.a. the Red Lake Volcano, and take in the full scale of the place. There is an enormous lake – four times the size of an Olympic swimming pool – with two smaller lakes to the side. It really is the most spectacular, and almost outlandish, sight.

Down by the side of the largest body of water are the remains of the engine house, which contained a steam-plant, used to pump water out as the clay was mined. The clay itself was washed before being sent down a pipeline to Bittaford, on the southern edge of the moor. There was also a hostel here where the workers lived during the week, which was run by a Mr and Mrs Bray. However the clay they dug here turned out not to be as fine as they had hoped, and the enterprise, known as the China Clay Corporation, went bust in 1932. The railway track was lifted soon afterwards, but fascinatingly, up until the 1960s, according to Eric Hemery (in *High Dartmoor*), people used to drive along the old track in their cars. Eventually the authorities put a stop to this. Can you imagine fleets of cars parked by Red Lake now?

The three pools are quite simply a swimmer's paradise. In summer they are warm and inviting, but they are magical in winter too - desolate, remote and dark. It feels like swimming on the edge of the world. You can get a really long swim in the big lake, but the smaller pools are fun to explore too, and are lined in the summer with delicate bog cotton, with wispy white flowers like sheeps' tails.

The remoteness of Red Lake means you'll be pretty exhausted by the time you get there.

It's really good fun to camp – as well as being a welcome chance for a lie down after that massive hike – but make sure you take precautions against midges. Whether you stay the night or return the same day, once you get back to civilisation the memory of these isolated lakes, in the middle of such a stark, unforgiving landscape, will stay with you for quite some time.

DIRECTIONS

1 From Harford Gate car park, follow the path north east until it links up with the Two Moors Way. Follow the Two Moors Way north until you get to Leftlake, which is on the path. It is a good wide path which follows the high ground above the Erme valley.
3.3 miles

2 From Leftlake, follow the Two Moors Way for another three miles until you get to a pyramid shaped marker stone – which marks the start of the Red Lake Tramway heading north.
2.3 miles

3 Keep ahead on the Tramway – not the Two Moors Way - for the last half mile to Red Lake.
0.7 miles

4 To return, retrace your steps. If you have the stamina or time you might like to return (or indeed ascend) via the Erme valley. You will need a good map and be prepared to do some serious exploring and bush-whacking. It adds on about three miles and several hours. Follow the course of the Red Lake stream west from Red Lake and pick up the northern end of the Erme stone row. Follow this for two miles to the dramatic stone circle then drop down to the river and follow this. You will pass a man-made weir plunge pool and arrive at Piles Copse where there is another pool. This is a popular camping spot. Follow the path south west for a mile up past the waterworks, and onto the lane to return via the lanes to Harford, via Tor.

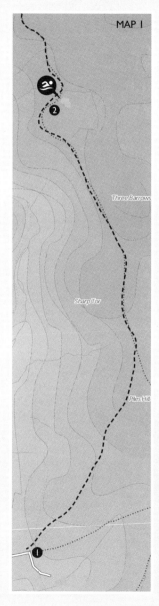

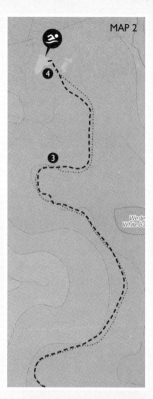

IVYBRIDGE POOLS CIRCULAR

The town of Ivybridge has a wonderful
secret – a series of delightful pools above
an impressive gorge, shaded by the magical
majesty of Longtimber Woods.

*I*t's worth starting your walk with a brief pause on
the original Ivy Bridge, watching the River Erme
wind its way through the gorge, racing towards its
destination at Mothecombe on the coast. The town
of Ivybridge owes its very existence to the river and the bridge,
which dates back to at least the 13th Century. While originally
only wide enough for pack horses, the crossing meant that the
town became a popular coaching stop for passing trade between
Exeter and Plymouth. Interestingly the bridge is the meeting
point of the boundaries of four parishes – Harford, Ugborough,
Ermington and Cornwood.

The river became a source for water-powered industry and by
the 16th century there was a tin mill, an edge mill and a corn mill
known as Glanville's Mill (now the name of the shopping centre
where it once stood). These mills were later joined by a tucking
mill for cloth-making and two paper mills, and just before you
enter the woods you'll pass the rear entrance of the old Stowford
Paper Mill dating back to 1862. The mill used to produce very
high quality paper, used for writing, as well as the production of
bank notes, but sadly closed in 2013.

Entering Longtimber Woods is truly magical, as you instantly
find yourself overlooking the River Erme as it tumbles through
the ravine below the old millworks and the grottos it has carved,
known as the 'doglegs' by canoeists. Don't be tempted to swim
here though - far better treats await you above the spectacular
viaduct that will soon come into view. Passing under the towering
industrial structure and past a pool ominously known as Danger
Wall, you'll discover pillars which once carried the original

wooden viaduct, built by Isambard Kingdom Brunel to become part of his impractical atmospheric railway. Take a slight deviation to the right of the main path, and about 50 metres upstream you'll find the far more romantically named Lovers Pool, popular with local youngsters who enjoy jumping into the long, deep swimming hole.

Carrying on upstream another 150 metres you'll find a much sunnier pool known as Head Weir ❷ and the former intake for the paper mill on the opposite side. A footbridge once crossed the river a little downstream from here, although today the only way to cross it is to take a dip. And why not? This is a wonderful swimming spot with a small bubbly waterfall at the top end, and a small rock island in the middle, crying out to be conquered. This stretch of water is popular with grey wagtails and dippers of a feathered variety, as well as an abundance of fish.

Talking of wildlife, this track besides the river was once a drovers' road to and from the moor and you'll spot the walls of several old animal pounds to your left. You'll also spot the remains of an old overgrown swimming pool, adapted from an old reservoir. This was apparently once popular with children, before being commandeered by American troops for training exercises prior to D-Day. The soldiers even apparently carried sand to the pool to turn it into a beach for themselves and the youngsters of Ivybridge. Salute their courage before continuing along to a fork in the path that leads to a riverside picnic spot.

This stretch of the Erme is the watery grail for swimmers in the area – the simply enchanting Trinnaman's Pool ❸. A rather dark Dartmoor legend tells how the pool once took the life of a murderous butler called John Trinnaman, but

innocent wild swimmers should be safe. Another legend concerns the ghost of a white bull who roams the woods around here. Whenever the creature appears, a death is supposed to be about to occur in the family – but we can't help but think it's a load of bull!

Enter the circular pool near the tree trunk and the old tinners' mortar stone, and enjoy a refreshing swim upstream against the current. The pool is fed by a wonderful little waterfall that creates a natural jacuzzi below, and is framed perfectly by overhanging trees to create an idyllic scene that even the most talented of artists would struggle to conjure up from their own imaginations. Above the waterfall, there are even more treats waiting to be discovered. Zulu (again named by kayakers) is a long and narrow 'Cresta Run' of a pool, with almost unnaturally straight sides and fed by yet another small waterfall. It's perfect for some wet-suited 'whooshing' during the winter months.

The path pulls away from the river into Pithill Wood, before you climb up a set of steps and bend back on yourself to follow a higher path with glimpses of the moor through the trees. Soon the eerie silence is broken by the babble of the Erme below as you continue through the lush woodland, with light glinting through the canopy above. The path is suspiciously quiet and you'll discover why if you continue straight on at the next sign post. This path gets really wet and muddy at certain times of the year, and we found ourselves climbing up onto one of the banks above (where it was much dryer) to continue the adventure. Look out for the remains of old quarries along the route, which gave Pithill its name and provided building materials for the town.

Eventually you come out onto a lane near Pithill Farm. While you can continue straight back down to the viaduct, we'd recommend turning right through the metal gate and up onto Henlake Down ❺. The route circumnavigates the gorse-covered down, with breathtaking views up onto the open moors and further on right down to the coast and the sea. Once you have walked up past the silver birch, pause on the railway sleeper bench for atmospheric views right up to the granite outcrop at Western Beacon.

As well as trees crying out to be climbed, the down also hides prehistoric remains and once even boasted a racecourse. The track was created by the Rogers family, who were the principal landowners in the 18th century. Indeed Dame Hannah Rogers even left a £10,000 legacy in 1767 to set up a school in Ivybridge that is still running today. The Dame Hannah Rogers Trust supports children with often profound disabilities, and remains very much at the heart of Ivybridge.

Eventually you will return to the lane that takes you back under the viaduct down to the Ivy Bridge. There is a tiny entrance just before the viaduct on your right that will take you up to where the old platform of the railway was, if you have time and are feeling curious. It's then back over the bridge and to the car park, where you can't have failed to notice a large piece of equipment we've heard described as both a giant snail and a huge vintage hair dryer. There's no sign to explain what it is, but as you might have guessed it's actually a water turbine that was once installed at the corn mill. By day the 22 foot water wheel powered the mill and by night this turbine produced electricity for Ivybridge itself. Another graphic reminder of how important and intertwined the river is in the history of this town.

1 From the car park, walk up Harford Road, turning left to cross Ivy Bridge. Then turn right up Station Road and past the old entrance of the paper mill, entering the woods on the public footpath. Note there is some free additional parking here. Follow the river upstream and under the viaduct. Turn right straight after passing under the viaduct and down to the river for an optional swim at Lovers Pool.
0.5 miles

2 From Lovers Pool carry along the main path another five minutes to reach a second possible swimming spot at Head Weir. Continue along the path looking out for the old stone gateposts and walls of the former reservoir/swimming pool. Just past the next public footpath sign, turn right down to the river by the notice board and picnic table, and you will shortly find Trinnaman's Pool by which is a large tree stump and an old tinner's mortice stone.
0.3 miles

3 From Trinnaman's Pool, return to the path and continue walking upstream until you eventually reach a stile at King's Corner. There is an option here to cross the stile and continue up to see the church at Harford, adding 2.2 miles to the walk. Otherwise do not cross the stile, but instead turn left up the steep steps.
0.5 miles

4 Go up the steps and follow the path to the left through the trees. At the next signpost it is possible to take a left back down towards the river (a good idea if there has been lots of rain and the path ahead is likely to be muddy). Otherwise walk straight on along the old low-walled path past the old quarry on your right and eventually out onto the lane.
0.7 miles

5 You then have the highly recommended option of extending the walk with a stroll around Henlake Down. To do this, turn right through the unmarked metal gate with the granite post. Bear right and follow the footpath that circumnavigates the down in an anti-clockwise direction, eventually exiting back out onto the same lane.
1 mile

6 Continue down the lane

towards the viaduct. At the bottom of the hill, turn left over the old bridge and then right back to the car park.
0.4 miles

Great Mattiscombe Sand

South Devon

Walk 15

MOUNT BATTEN PENINSULA CIRCULAR

An unusual walk taking in the fascinating maritime history of Britain's Ocean City, with amazing views of Plymouth Sound and plenty of swims along the way

INFORMATION

DISTANCE: 2.5 miles
TIME: 2-3 hours
MAP: OS Explorer South Devon OL20
START POINT: Jennycliff Car Park (SX 492 523, PL9 9SW)
END POINT: Jennycliff Car Park
PUBLIC TRANSPORT: From Plymouth catch the First Devon and Cornwall service 2 to Hooe Road and then it's an 8 minute walk to Jennycliff. In the summer the 54 bus service runs directly to Jennycliff from the city centre. You can also take the ferry across from the Barbican and start and finish the walk from there
SWIMMING: Batten Bay (SX 488 530), Clovelly Bay (SX 493 531), Hooe Lake (SX 497 527)
PLACES OF INTEREST: Mount Batten Tower, the Breakwater, Mount Batten Peninsula, Turnchapel, Hooe Lake
REFRESHMENTS: Jennycliff Café serves hearty breakfasts and delicious fish and chips, all served with incredible views (01752 402358, PL9 9SW). The Clovelly Bay Inn is a very popular village inn in Turnchapel, renowned for its food and ales, and with a beach on the doorstep (01752 402765, PL9 9TB)

oday's walk starts from Jennycliff car park, which boasts impressive views across Plymouth Sound on a clear day. From left to right you should be able to see the Plymouth Breakwater, the headland at Penlee Point and the villages of Kingsand and Cawsand in Cornwall, Mount Edgcumbe Country Park, Drakes Island, the Tamar Estuary and Plymouth Hoe. Jennycliff itself takes its name from the jennies (female donkeys) which once grazed here. The walk takes you down past the café and past a large South West Coast Path marker stone. These large white stones signify you have also joined Plymouth's Waterfront Walkway, a 9.3 mile trail featuring art works and interpretation boards illustrating the city's rich heritage.

Once you have paused at the benches on the headland above Rum Bay for yet more wonderful views, the path takes you past another marker stone and down to Batten Bay ❷. This is a great swim spot at high tide and also a popular place for rock pooling and crabbing at low tide when the rocks are exposed. Look out for the velvet swimming crab with red eyes and aggressive fighting tactics! The views as you swim out are wonderful, while there are some rocky gullies to explore off to the right, where you might also spot shags and oyster catchers.

The bay is also popular with snorkellers, with a limestone reef offshore, as well as eelgrass beds and even shipwrecks. There's plenty to spot in the water below, including seahorses, pink sea fan, dead man's fingers, sea slugs, sea cucumbers, crabs, anemones and pipefish. Incidentally if you do see a large dorsal fin in the waters during the summer months, you may have spotted the

second largest species of shark in the world. Don't worry, it's only a plankton-eating Basking Shark.

After your swim, the walk continues past the bay and up the hill to the Mount Batten Tower. The Mount Batten Peninsula (or Howe Stert as it was known before the Civil War) is almost certainly the oldest settlement in Plymouth. There was a thriving community here from at least 1000 BC until the Roman era, as many Bronze and Iron Age artefacts have been discovered here. The tower itself dates to the 1650s and the Dutch Wars, and is named after Vice Admiral Captain Batten, who commanded the naval forces defending the peninsula during the English Civil War. The tower remained in defence use until the 1770s and was later used as a naval and coastguard look-out and signal tower. The tower is only open to the public on special occasions, but the views from the hill are magnificent.

Steps take you down to the Mount Batten Breakwater ❸ and another marker stone engraved with the image of a seaplane and a hint at the area's history. The peninsula was used for seaplane trials in the early days of the Royal Naval Air Service, which established a seaplane station here in 1917 to defend the South West. This became RAF Cattewater and was renamed RAF Mount Batten in 1928 at the suggestion of one Aircraftman Shaw, better known as TE Lawrence (Lawrence of Arabia), who was stationed here. The base became particularly active during the Second World War, when it also became the target for German air raids. Post-war it became a maintenance unit and later an RAF School of Combat Survival and the Marine Branch for Air/Sea Rescue. The RAF sold Mount Batten in 1992 and the area was redeveloped as a recreational area and centre for water sports.

There are great views from here across to The Hoe, which is Plymouth's waterfront park, with its iconic red and white lighthouse, Smeaton's Tower. The lighthouse was moved here from the Eddystone Rocks when it was replaced with a new lighthouse in 1882. Just slightly to the left of the lighthouse you should also be able to spot the renovated Art Deco Tinside Lido jutting out into the water. The Plymouth members of Devon and Cornwall Wild Swimmers meet here for swims throughout the year, on the steps by Tinside Beach.

The walk continues past the Mount Batten Pier, where you can catch a ferry across to the historic Barbican. This charming area is home to the Mayflower Steps where the Pilgrim Fathers set sail on their voyage to the New World in 1620. The Barbican is also home to the National Marine Aquarium and, more importantly, Plymouth Gin! Look across to the right before you pass the Hotel Mount Batten and you will spot a replica of the propeller of a Sunderland flying boat. The slipway you pass is the starting point of the swim section of the annual Plymouth Triathlon.

As you continue around the peninsula you will spot code words embedded in the walkway. In the early 20th century, seafarers would use telegraphs to communicate with those back home. However, they were charged by the word, meaning a long message could become very expensive. To get around this problem, Captain DH Barnard devised *The Nautical Telegraph Code* in which one word stood for a particular message. The messages can be found all along Plymouth's Waterfront Walkway, although you'll need a copy of the book to uncover the meanings.

The walk continues past the Mount Batten Centre for water sports and alongside the Cattewater, which is the estuary of the River Plym. The path

then winds through a boat yard and into the Yacht Haven area, an impressive marina in the shelter of Clovelly Bay. After walking up the steps, you then drop back down into the olde-worlde village of Turnchapel, ❹ with funky colourful buildings including the Clovelly Bay Inn. This popular pub has two entrances, one advertising Ales and the other Vittles and is well worth a refreshment stop. There's also a small beach in front of the pub, should you fancy a different type of refreshment.

Next you'll pass Turnchapel Wharf, which was the former home of 539 Royal Marines Assault Squadron and is now a waterfront site for various marine businesses including Princess Yachts. You'll then turn right alongside Hooe Lake ❺, a tidal creek off the Plym Estuary. The four pillars in the water once carried a railway from Plymouth to Turnchapel when it was a thriving centre for shipbuilding and repair. At low tide the decaying hulks of a several old boats can be spotted in the creek, making for great photo opportunities. It's also lovely to swim here at high tide, from the small beach halfway along. At the end of the creek a dam separates Hooe Lake from freshwater Radford Lake and you'll be able to spot a folly built in the early 19th century, known as Radford Castle.

After a short stint walking up the hill along pavements and past some uninspiring architecture, you'll soon turn onto a welcome grassy path which leads you back up to the car park. Jennycliff Beach, about a five minute walk from the car park is another lovely place for a final swim, but at the time of writing it was closed due to cliff falls. Looking out over this green clifftop, it's easy to forget how close to a major city you are. But Plymouth bills itself as 'Britain's Ocean City' for a reason, and this unusual swim walk has certainly proved why.

DIRECTIONS

1 From the car park at Jennycliff walk in front of the café across the grassy area to the right towards the stone with the acorn symbol on it, and onto the South West Coast Path. Follow the path around the headland above Rum Bay, past the benches to another stone marked South, then towards the wooden footpath sign in the bottom corner of the field. Follow the hedged path down and then left onto the pavement.
0.5 miles

2 Turn left down the wooden steps and onto the beach for a swim stop at Batten Bay. Following the swim, walk back up the wooden steps and turn left along the pavement and then turn left at the Breakwater sign. Then go up the hill to Mount Batten. The steps then take you down towards the Breakwater.
0.3 miles

3 Walk past the waymarker stone with the aeroplane on it and along the waterside path past the foot ferry. The path now curves along the Cattewater (the estuary of the River Plym), past the Mount Batten Centre for water sports and through the boat yard. Turn left down past the metal buoys and follow the Coast Path signs for Turnchapel, winding through the Yacht Haven area. At the top of the steps turn left and then left again, past the blue plaque for TE Lawrence and down into Turnchapel and the Clovelly Bay Inn. There is another potential swim spot from the beach in front of the pub.
0.7 miles

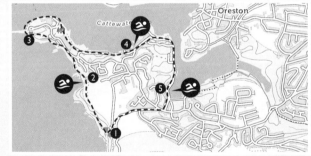

4 Continue through Turnchapel, then right at the end and past Princess Yachts. At the end turn right along the tidal creek past the old railway bridge supports into Hooe Lake. There are several places along here you can enter the water for a swim at high tide.
0.4 miles

5 Continue along the side of the lake, then turn right onto Hooe Road and then left onto Jennycliff Lane. Walk up the hill and then turn left onto the grassy track and back up to Jennycliff Car Park.
0.5 miles

CELLAR BEACH CIRCULAR

This is a simply gorgeous walk and swim, taking in huge and rugged cliffs, with vertiginous and far-reaching views, as well as the softer scenery of the Yealm estuary.

INFORMATION

DISTANCE: 4.5 miles
TIME: 2 hours
MAP: OS Explorer South Devon OL20
START POINT: Car park by the tennis courts in Noss Mayo (PL8 1EH, SX 547 474)
END POINT: Car park by the tennis courts in Noss Mayo
PUBLIC TRANSPORT: Number 94 Bus from Plymouth. Mon-Sat
SWIMMING: Cellar Beach (SX 531 475) River Yealm estuary at Kilpatrick Steps (SX 540 477)
PLACES OF INTEREST: Revelstoke Drive, Cellar Beach which is sandy at low tide
REFRESHMENTS: The Ship Inn, Noss Mayo has a lovely setting overlooking the harbour with wooden floors and log fires in winter. It also has fun, clear 'pods' you can sit in outside, enjoying the views while staying warm (01752 872387, PL8 1EW). Also the Swan Inn (01752 872392, PL8 1EE). At low tide you can walk across to the Dolphin Inn in Newton Ferrers (01752 872007, PL8 1AE)

*C*ellar Beach is an idyllic place to dip, and, if you're feeling a bit more energetic, you can swim up the estuary to the pub in the village. The walk starts in the picturesque village of Noss Mayo ❶, which clusters around a creek of the Yealm estuary. Its origins go back to the 13th century, and there is an unusual story about the name. Apparently King Edward I gave the manor to a fellow called Mathew Fitzjohn, and so it became known as Noss Mayo – Mathew's nose. Maybe he really did have a notable nose, or perhaps, more prosaically, the name refers to the promontory on which the village sits.

The first part of the walk is the hardest, as you ascend from the village, past fields and the odd cottage, to the coast path ❸. Once here, it's pretty much flat or downhill the rest of the way. On the coast path, the views are absolutely spectacular, both downwards to the craggy and tantalisingly inaccessible coves below, and out to sea, where you should be able to see the Eddystone Lighthouse on a clear day. You walk along a wide path known as Revelstoke's Drive. It was created by Edward Baring, a Victorian financier and Director of the Bank of England, who had his country estate here, and took the name Lord Revelstoke when he was made a Baron. He built the drive so he could enjoy the panoramic views from the comfort of his horse-drawn carriage. The first headland you reach, Blackstone Point, has a wall around it, which was built to prevent the horses from tumbling down the cliffs below.

As you walk around from Blackstone Point, you will see a picturesque cottage ahead, right on the coast path. This is Warren Cottage ❹, which Lord Revelstoke used as a tea house for summer parties. What fun it must have been to travel out in the carriage

along the top of the cliffs, before stopping for a huge spread - no doubt taken out by the servants in advance. It's even rumoured that the future Edward VII took tea here.

As you continue to walk along the coast path, you will see a triangular shaped island. This is the Mewstone, which, amazingly, was inhabited in Victorian times by a series of individuals, the last of whom was called Samuel Wakeham, who lived there with his wife Anne, some chickens, some pigs and lots of rabbits. Apparently it was quite a popular destination for day trippers from Plymouth, who would pay a crown to go out in a boat and call on Sam on the island. He even took the trouble to carve steps in the rocks, to assist the ladies as they came ashore.

The path continues bearing north towards the estuary, with beautiful views down to inlets and lagoons below. At the mouth of the estuary is a sandbar. There's a local tradition of playing cricket there on the rare occasions when there are very low spring tides, when it's exposed just long enough for a quick game!

Cellar Beach ❼ is just inside the mouth of the estuary, and at high tide it gets covered by water. It doesn't matter, as there is a huge rocky outcrop which soaks up the sun and is a great place to sit and relax; it's also good to swim off. The name Cellar is thought to refer to the temporary storage buildings the fishermen used to build on the beach, to house their equipment. You may notice that the locals refer to it as Cellars Beach. This is because its original name was 'Old Cellars Beach'.

It is enormous fun to swim from Cellar Beach up the estuary to The Ship Inn in Noss Mayo. It's a distance of about 1½ miles, but do use the incoming tide to help you. The tidal push

is strongest three-four hours after low water. Alternatively, for a shorter but equally enjoyable swim, you can get in at Kilpatrick Steps, just past the cluster of houses around the old Toll House, further along on the walk (see below), or indeed at any point along the estuary where you can get in. It is important to wear a bright swimming cap so you can be seen by the many boats in the estuary.

This swim is particularly magical. When you're being moved along by the incoming tide, it's a bit like flying as you whizz over the seabed below. The water is usually clear and you may see shoals of sand eel, as well as bass and mullet. As you get further up the estuary, it's apparent that it's a haven for people who love 'messing about in boats', and you'll pass all manner of craft. The Yealm is home to a particular sort of sailing boat, the Drascombe, which was designed by John Watkinson in the 1960s. These boats were first built in a yard in the village, and have an enthusiastic following; the Drascombe Association describes them as "simple, rugged and seakindly".

If you do go for the estuary swim there will hopefully be walkers in the party to carry your stuff on to Noss Mayo. The final part of the walk, which pretty much goes alongside the swim, involves taking the path back up from Cellar Beach, and continuing along through exceptionally pretty woods, with beautiful views through the trees to the estuary below. You pass the Toll House for the original Yealm Ferry; the old toll sign is still there. It cost you three old pence to take a 'horse or an ass' on the ferry, and one penny for a bag of potatoes. Just after the Toll House and other houses around it you will pass Kilpatrick Steps on your left, another lovely swim spot.

The path becomes a single track road, which continues through the woods alongside the estuary, and finishes in the village by The Ship. This pub does a particularly good line in hot chocolate, with squirty cream on top, perfect for warming up after the swim!

❶ From the car park, turn left up the lane, with the houses on your right.
0.1 miles

❷ The lane turns into a track. There is a sign saying No Through Road; keep following the track.
0.5 miles

❸ After about 20 minutes the path hits a road, you will see a gate straight ahead with a sign saying Coastal Footpath and Worswell Farm. Turn left along the road and soon right by a car park. There is a sign saying Public Footpath / Coast Path. You get to a gate which says Keep Dogs Under Control – go through here, turn right and follow the coast path west with the sea on your left.
0.5 miles

❹ Follow the path past Warren Cottage, and keep going.
0.7 miles

❺ Follow the path around the headland at the mouth of the estuary and follow it into the woods with the estuary on your left.
0.2 miles

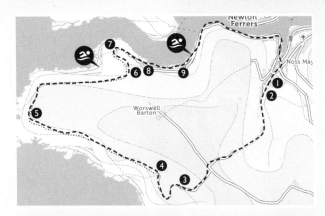

❻ Once out of the woods, you pass a valley with fields and a stream on your left, and then get to some cottages on your right.
0.5 miles

❼ It is easy to miss the turning down to Cellar Beach. It's on the left, opposite a large Arts and Crafts style house, which has a weather vane with a ship on it. There is a small wooden sign with the yellow National Trust acorn on it, saying Cellar Beach. Take this left hand turning off the main path and follow it down to the beach.
670 feet

❽ Coming back up from the beach, turn left at the Arts and Crafts house and follow the path. Just past the gate and a parking area on the left, there's a path to the left going down into the woods. Take this path.
0.2 miles

❾ Follow the path behind the cottages and the Toll House and past Kilpatrick Steps (another swim spot). Keep going and you will pick up a road which takes you along the estuary and back to the village.
1.1 miles

Walk 17

WESTCOMBE AND WONWELL CIRCULAR

This is an exciting and quite strenuous walk, taking in an old smugglers' village, fascinating caves and rock formations, a wooded estuary and two swimming beaches.

T he walk starts by the Church of St James the Less ❶ in the heart of the village of Kingston, and immediately you pass the historic Dolphin Inn, which dates back to the 16th century. Note the images of dolphins everywhere, even over the sign to the gents! You head out of the village down a track, which can be extremely muddy, passing fishing lakes and, unusually, a willow plantation. The fishermen of the village traditionally made their lobster and crab pots out of willow and it is interesting to see it is still being grown today. This track would no doubt have been used by fishermen to get to the beach, and indeed smugglers too!

When you get to Westcombe Beach ❸ you'll see a dilapidated building on your left. It's the remains of old stables, built to accommodate the horses belonging to the local landowners the Mildmays, of the Flete estate. They would frequently drive their carriages to local beaches for parties, including to Westcombe, where they had a tea house (which sadly no longer remains). It's even rumoured that members of the Royal Family were among their guests. A pamphlet about the history of the village, published in 1987, records the reminiscences of villager Ivy Willcocks, who died in 1987. Ivy describes how the then carriageway down to the beach was "kept beautiful and trimmed and cleared up….they used to bring the servants to wait on them and all, it was wonderful for us kids to see them."

The beach is spectacular, with rugged and intricate rock formations, and distinctive grey sand, reflecting the slate in the cliffs. At low tide, to the right, you can make your way through the rocks to another beach where there are extensive and intriguing caves,

INFORMATION

DISTANCE: 5 miles
TIME: 3 hours
MAP: OS Explorer South Devon OL20
START POINT: St James the Less Church, Kingston. Park in the village outside the church (SX 635 478, TQ7 4QB)
END POINT: St James the Less Church, Kingston
PUBLIC TRANSPORT: On Fridays only, the 875 from Plymouth. However, it is impractical as it will not allow enough time to do the walk
SWIMMING: Westcombe Beach (SX 635 457) and Wonwell Beach (SX 617 472)
PLACES OF INTEREST: St James the Less Church, Westcombe Beach caves, Wonwell Beach and estuary
REFRESHMENTS: The Dolphin Inn at Kingston is a 16th century pub which also does bed and breakfast (01548 810314, TQ7 4QE). In the next village, Ringmore, is another nice pub, the Journey's End, which has some cosy nooks to sit in, and good food (01548 810205, TQ7 4HL)

many linked to each other. Rumour has it these were used by smugglers, and some even say there was a tunnel all the way from the caves through to Scobbiscombe Farm inland.

At high tide, if it's calm, you can swim through and in and out of the numerous rocky channels. You can also swim over the extensive reefs, admiring unusual anemones including the strawberry and snakelocks varieties. You can often see oyster catchers here too and, if you're really lucky, a peregrine falcon.

After a thorough exploration of Westcombe Beach, you face a tough ascent along the coast path heading west. At the top you have stunning views of Burgh Island to the east, and further along you reach Beacon Point, one of the places where huge fires have been lit to mark important events over the years. Apparently the first to be lit here was in Elizabethan times, to warn of the Spanish Armada.

You then reach the Erme estuary, one of South Devon's prettiest, with lovely Wonwell Beach ❹ at the mouth. This is very much a locals beach as it involves a winding drive through narrow lanes, with very few passing places, to get to it by car. Over on the other side you can see a row of old coastguard cottages, where they tried to keep a lid on all the smuggling activities. Before the First World War, coal would be brought in here in barges from Wales, which would keep Kingston supplied for a year.

It's a lovely swimming spot, with views out to sea and across to Mothecombe on the other side. At low tide you may need to wade quite a way to get out of your depth! The estuary is totally unspoilt and you may see herons, egrets and cormorants. It is a truly peaceful place, and constantly changing, according to what the tide is doing. When it's low

you can walk a long way up the river, past old lime kilns, and if you get far enough you can see across to Efford House on the other side, one of the locations in Ang Lee's 1995 film *Sense and Sensibility*; the house played the role of the Dashwood family's Devon 'cottage'.

The walk finishes by ascending up through beautiful woods, full of wild garlic and bluebells in spring, and back through fields to the village.

DIRECTIONS

❶ From the church, walk down the lane with the Dolphin Inn on your right. Turn right at the T junction and then left at Rock Cottages. Follow the track down the hill. Bear left at the fork marked Jarfin.
0.2 miles

❷ At the next fork bear right along the bridleway (don't take the footpath to Ringmore). Continue to follow the track to Westcombe Beach.
1.5 miles

❸ From the beach follow the coast path west to the Erme estuary and Wonwell Beach.
2.3 miles

❹ At Wonwell Beach, if it's low tide, you can walk up the sand and then up the slipway to the lane. If it's high tide, follow the coast path above the beach and through the wood until you get to the bottom of the lane.
0.3 miles

❺ Walk up the lane and then

turn right through the woods, following the public footpath signposted Kingston.
0.3 miles

❻ Once out of the woods follow the footpath through the fields until it hits the lane. Turn right here and then left at the end of the lane, and you will find yourself back at the church.
0.7 miles

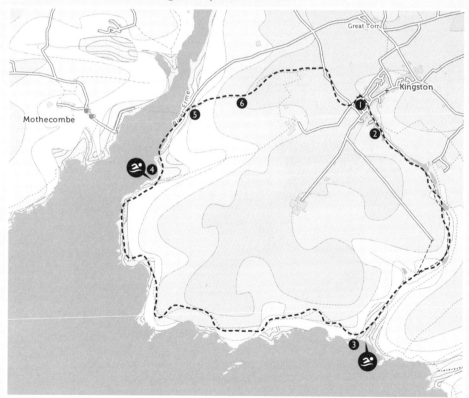

BANTHAM TO THURLESTONE CIRCULAR

This short walk takes in abundant wildlife, magnificent cliff-top views and a selection of beaches perfect for dippers or more serious swimmers.

*B*antham is a popular beach on one of the most beautiful stretches of coast in the UK, with views across Bigbury Bay to Burgh Island and its iconic Art Deco hotel. Understandably popular with both surfers and swimmers alike, the beach is nestled at the mouth of the River Avon and can be found at the base of marram grass-covered sand dunes.

Our walk takes us from the car park where generations of surfers have gathered whenever the rumour of a swell from the south brought the promise of sizeable waves. Once you have climbed up the slope from Bantham Surf Life Saving Club, it's worth pausing at the bench to take in the charming tidal island just a stone's skip away in the distance. Cut off by the tide twice a day, it oozes romance and mystery. It's no surprise that Agatha Christie used the island as the inspirational setting for two of her most popular books, *Evil Under the Sun* and the oft-renamed *And Then There Were None*.

According to local folklore, back in the 20s and 30s, floating cocktail bars were moored in summer at various points offshore for swimmers. The hotel always used to run an annual round-the-island swimming race, with drinks served to the winners by waiters in black tie. We took part in the last one, in 2012, which was a wonderfully glamorous and eccentric occasion. Sadly, after that, it became too much of an insurance headache for the hotel, and the annual tradition ended. The mile-long circumnavigation, past imposing cliffs, rocky inlets and mysterious coves remains popular with swimmers, although currents and choppy waters can make for a bold swim and caution is advised.

INFORMATION

DISTANCE: 4 miles
TIME: 3–4 hours
MAP: OS Explorer South Devon OL20
START POINT: Bantham car park (SX 663 436, TQ7 3AN)
END POINT: Bantham car park
PUBLIC TRANSPORT: Seasonal passenger ferry to Bigbury. Nearest train stations are Totnes (17 Miles) or Ivybridge (14 Miles). There are no buses to Bantham, but you can reach Thurlestone on the 162 Tally Ho! service which runs from Kingsbridge
SWIMMING: Bantham Sands (SX 662 437), South Milton Sands (SX 676 417), Leas Foot Sand (SX 673 421)
PLACES OF INTEREST: Bantham Village, Thurlestone Village, Thurlestone Arch
REFRESHMENTS: The Beach House at South Milton Sands does amazing seafood but is always busy so best to book (01548 561144, TQ7 3JY). The Sloop at Bantham is a comfy pub with good food (01548 560489, TQ7 3AJ). You can also eat at the Village Inn in Thurlestone which makes a good stop ¾ of the way round (01548 563525, TQ7 3NN), and there is the brilliant Gastrobus in the car park at Bantham which does a great line in quality 'fast food' (07592 811277, TQ7 3AN)

As the walk continues you'll pass Thurlestone Golf Club, which must have some of the most dramatic views of any course in the world. On a clear day you can see across to the headland of Bolt Tail to the east and Plymouth Sound to the west. You might even be able to make out the Eddystone Lighthouse and the stump of Smeaton's Tower (the main lighthouse was moved to Plymouth Hoe) some nine miles out to sea in front of you. This stretch of coast is a haven for bird lovers: regular visitors include rock pipits, pied wagtails and wheatears, as well as buzzards and kestrels.

The walk takes you right past the ninth hole and close to another bench, which is well worth pausing at. Dedicated to Bill Bennett, it includes a verse that combines quotes from Shakespeare and Dryden and clearly shows his passion for both the sea and life itself:

"*His delights were dolphin like*
Joy ruled the day and love the night"

From the bench you can see a cove below and we'd recommend a scramble down to this secret beach, which is wonderful for rock-pooling on a low tide. Back on the coast path the next small headland is known as Loam Castle, 'loam' being a high quality earth combing sand, clay and decaying plant material. You'll then reach Yarmouth Sand, another popular swim spot - the best area to take a dip to avoid submerged rocks is directly out from the sandy path that leads down to the beach, near the lifebuoy.

Continue on around the perimeter of the golf course and Warren Point for the first glimpse of Thurlestone Rock, an imposing rock arch that was immortalised by JMW Turner. The iconic natural sculpture was originally known as the 'Thirled Stone' from an Anglo-Saxon word meaning 'hole'. Before reaching South Milton Sands (formerly known as Thurlestone Sand, but controversially renamed, much to the consternation of locals), you'll pass Leas Foot Sand ❸. It's the smaller of Thurlestone's two beaches and owned by the golf club, with fine shingle sand. Part of the lane was swept into the sea here during the big storms of February 2014.

Walk down through the car park and onto South Milton Sands ❹, which has a small natural swimming pond that forms on the higher part of the beach at low tide. Many swimmers plan to get here at high tide however, so they can walk to the southern part of the beach and swim out to and through the arch, which sits at the end of a reef about 500 metres from the shore.

The swim out to the arch is stunning. At high water, the reef on which it stands is covered, and to swim over it is like being in a natural history film. Brightly coloured seaweed and darting fish create a colourful marine garden below you, while the arch itself makes the perfect natural picture frame to take in the magnificence of this wonderful section of coastline.

For the return part of the walk, retrace your steps back to Leas Foot Sand and turn right up the sand path at the start of the beach. You'll pass four stone slabs known as the Fool Stones. Legend has it that if you kiss each of the stones from right to left you can make a wish! Continue through the grass overflow car park and left into the main car park, towards the club house. There are public toilets on your right. Follow the road past the tennis courts and on up the hill, walking up the raised pavement on the left.

In Thurlestone Village itself, you'll reach the war memorial and be able to spot the post office to your right, which is ideal for refreshments. The red phone box has been converted into a charming mini library. It's also just a short stroll to the 16th century Village Inn (a separate part of the Thurlestone Hotel) with beams salvaged from Spanish Armada ships, wrecked on the nearby coast.

The walk continues up past the memorial and then right, following the sign for Footpath to Bantham and past All Saints Church, built from local dark grey slate. The walk takes you over a stile, past the rear of the golf course and across several fields, before you are rewarded with spectacular views over the estuary below. Another popular swim adventure is to walk or drive up to Aveton Gifford and then swim the three miles down to Bantham with the tide. This swim finishes with a 'swoosh' where the estuary narrows, allowing you to swim at eight knots, or four times faster than normal. The Outdoor Swimming Society organises an annual Bantham Swoosh event.

Head down the fields and through a stile in the hedge, before a really steep field leads you back into the village near the 14th century Sloop Inn. It's worth a stop for a well-earned drink or bite to eat. An amusing local story goes that you used to be able to tell whether a man came from Bantham or Thurlestone by looking at his trousers. A man with a patch on them came from Bantham and those with no patch came from the nearby village. How did they know? The Sloop Inn boasted benches for its customers while, the Village Inn at Thurlestone had none!

DIRECTIONS

❶ From the bottom left hand corner of Bantham Sands car park take the road towards the beach and the Surf Life Saving Club, forking left at the bottom to go through the kissing gate and onto the South West Coast Path. It is signed for Thurlestone. Climb the slope and follow the path up to the point.
0.3 miles

❷ Follow the path along the cliff top. You go past several beaches which are swimmable, and then past the golf course on your left.
1.4 miles

❸ At Leas Foot Sand keep going along the coast path with the sea on your right, past the large block of apartments and then down to South Milton Sands for a swim and picnic. On a calm day and at high tide, some swimmers like to try and swim through the rock arch. The arch also marks the end of a reef that runs parallel to the shore which is great for snorkelling.
0.3 miles

❹ From South Milton Sand, return to the start of Leas Foot Sand and then turn right up the sand path, through the overflow parking field and left into the main golf club car park. Continue up onto the road to Thurlestone past the golf club and tennis courts on your left. Continue up the hill to the war memorial, perhaps pausing in the village for refreshments. **0.9 miles**

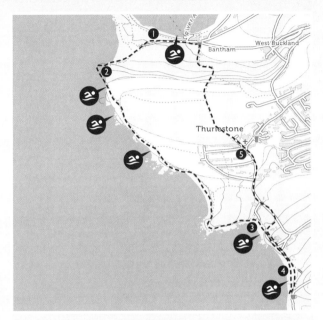

❺ At the war memorial leave the road and continue straight on along a track signed Public Footpath Bantham 3/4 mile. Follow the waymarked path through several fields before descending steeply into the valley. After two stiles you will eventually come out onto the lane in Bantham, near the Sloop Inn. Follow the lane back down to the car park.
0.9 miles

Walk 19

SOAR MILL COVE CIRCULAR

A spectacular swim walk taking in golden beaches, thatched hamlets, stunning clifftop walks and some of the most eccentric history you will ever stumble upon.

The walk begins at the sandy tidal beach of North Sands, just to the south of fashionable Salcombe. In fact the town has become so popular with wealthy yachty types, that the town has the highest property prices in the UK outside of central London, ahead even of Sandbanks in Dorset. Thankfully walking and swimming are free! As you climb up above the beach along Cliff Road, look back towards the ruins of Fort Charles, resembling something out of a Famous Five story. This was the last fort in England to hold out against Cromwell's men during the English Civil War of 1646.

The walk continues past the driveway to The Moult, a property that proves that Salcombe has been popular with the wealthy for hundreds of years. Recently on the market for 'offers over £5 Million', the villa on this private headland was built in the early 19th century around the core of an earlier house dating back to 1764. The town became very popular with rich Victorians, who came to holiday in what was regarded as the warmest resort on the south coast, and the house became the maritime residence of Viscount Courtenay, the Earl of Devon's eldest son. Famous guests included Alfred, Lord Tennyson, who stayed there shortly before his death in 1889. Legend has it he wrote his last poem, *Crossing the Bar*, an allegory to his own imminent death, while staying in the property's thatched summerhouse. Sadly the woods of beech and sycamore trees screen the house from prying eyes, meaning the historic house can only be seen from the water.

There are plenty of other desirable properties to view as you climb up the hill, before you eventually pass some bollards to enter the woods. The path then drops down onto a delightful

INFORMATION

DISTANCE: 6 miles
TIME: 4-5 hours
MAP: Ordnance Survey Explorer South Devon OL20
START POINT: North Sands car park (SX 730 382, TQ8 8LD)
END POINT: North Sands car park
PUBLIC TRANSPORT: Buses: the 606 from Kingsbridge and the 164 from Totnes
SWIMMING: Soar Mill Cove (SX 697 374), Starehole Bay (SX 726 365), North Sands (SX 730 381), South Sands (SX 728 376)
PLACES OF INTEREST: Overbecks (National Trust), Fort Charles, Starehole Bay
REFRESHMENTS: The Winking Prawn at North Sands is ideally positioned right by the beach. It's open all day with a good variety of 'surf and turf' (01548 842326, TQ8 8LD). The Soar Mill Hotel is a good halfway stop with nice cream teas (01548 561566, TQ7 3DS). For something a bit special with amazing views, check out the rather smart South Sands Hotel (01548 845900, TQ8 8LL).

country lane and up through a valley to the attractive thatched hamlet of Combe. Why not take a refreshment stop at the shady bench beside the stream and take a moment to read the charming inscription? It's then an energetic climb up the lane to Higher Rew Farm and a stunning campsite at a former dairy farm, which has been run by three generations of the Squire family.

The steep climb continues through fields above the camp site until you reach the former coastguard cottages at the aptly named hamlet of Soar. However the name has nothing to do with the elevation or the fact that there is an air strip nearby, but actually derives from an old English word for the plant sorrel. This is a herb with a sharp lemony flavour, which in turn derives from the French for 'sour'. The walk takes you past the rear of the five cottages, built in the 1870s, and then on to some barn conversions with chickens and ducks greeting you as you pass.

The path then takes you down past the curious looking Soar Mill Cove Hotel, a 22-bedroom four star hotel with an award-winning restaurant, a champagne bar and amazing spa facilities, including a seawater swimming pool. The hotel also has a remarkable history. The original building once housed a cinema at the Devonport Naval Base in Plymouth. The entire structure was then transported to the aerodrome near Rew during the Second World War, where it became an unofficial officers' mess. The building was then purchased from the navy and transported to Soar Mill Cove where it has been run as a hotel by the Makepeace family since 1978 (with several extensions added over the years). Incidentally if you do decide to dine here, save room for the pavlova, which was a favourite of Audrey Hepburn when she used to stay here.

It's then a stunning five minute walk down to the secluded sandy inlet, which owners the National Trust describe as one the best places in the UK for a picnic, and we're certainly not going to argue. If you're feeling adventurous, and only if you are a strong swimmer, you can swim around the Ham Stone, a small island off shore. A less daunting option, at high tide, is to swim around the Priest and Clerk rocks which cluster to the right of the beach (looking out to sea). There are also some wonderful caves to explore when the tide is out. One in particular goes back a long way and opens out into a dark, eerie cavern. At lower tides the beach is a rock pooling paradise, while look out for sea beet, rock samphire and the rare rock sea-lavender on the lower cliffs. Drying off on the beach after your swim, it's worth taking in the amazing moor-like hillsides above you, with granite outcrops resembling tors. Up to the right where the South West Coast Path continues, you can also spot the Iron Age fort remains, which was once a hillfort. It's a popular spot to sit at the close of a summer's day, watching out for dolphins and porpoises, or even gannets and peregrine falcons framed by the setting sun.

The walk back to Salcombe is along a remarkable stretch of the South West Coast Path, with some outstanding clifftop views. After ascending the hill from the beach, the path crosses another small valley before climbing up to one of the rugged tors. On a clear day you can see as far down the coast as Mewstone off Wembury, or even Plymouth Sound and the triangular shape of Rame Head in south-east Cornwall. The path then continues along a flat stretch of clifftop called The Warren. As the name suggests, this area was used to breed rabbits for their fur and meat back in medieval times. Today the area is managed by

the National Trust who use Dartmoor ponies to graze the cliffs, keeping the scrub under control so that wildlife and flowers can flourish.

The walk then continues around Bolt Head with amazing views across to Prawle Point, the most southerly point in Devon, before dropping down to beautiful Starehole Bay, another beautiful swimming spot. Be warned though, access was tricky last time we visited, because a footbridge which gives access to the beach had partly fallen away. We got down to the beach but it was a bit of a scramble. Apparently on a calm day you can spot the seaweed-covered wreck of the Herzogin Cecilie in the waters of the bay. This beautiful clipper had won the famous 'Grain Race' but it was the cargo that was to seal its fate. After running aground on the Ham Stone at Soar Mill Cove back in 1936, a rescue mission attempted to tow her back into Salcombe. However water entered the hold and the swollen grain split the timbers, and she sank in Starehole Bay. The wreck became a tourist attraction with local farmers charging a penny to view the wreck from their land. At very low tides, parts of her can still be seen above the surface, while timber and brass portholes salvaged from the ship can be found in the bar of the Cottage Hotel at Hope Cove.

Vikings are also said to have landed and settled in the bay sometime between the ninth and eleventh centuries. Indeed the jagged cliffs above you have been weathered into spires and crags and were dubbed 'Valhalla' by Henry Williamson, author of *Tarka the Otter*. It's possible to swim in Starehole Bay before climbing up to the rough-hewn steps and rocky ledges to round Sharptor, a remarkable route that wouldn't look

out of place in an Indiana Jones movie. This is known as Courtenay Walk and was cut in the 1860s by Viscount Courtenay, whose former house at The Moult we passed at the start of this walk.

The route now boasts stunning views over the entrance to Salcombe estuary, which, thanks to a sandbar extending just below the surface across the mouth, makes it notoriously hazardous to navigate. The estuary here is not actually fed by a river, but is a ria: a long narrow inlet formed when rising sea levels drown a valley. After walking through some woods, you'll find yourself in the car park of Overbecks, a National Trust property once owned by an eccentric chemist, collector and inventor called Otto Overbeck. He invented something called the 'electrical rejuvenator' which he claimed would allow people to live for 350 years. However it didn't work for him and he died in 1937, leaving the property to the National Trust on the condition it was turned into a museum and a youth hostel and not a brothel! Today the property is indeed divided between a YHA hostel and a museum of oddities he collected from around the world.

It's then down to South Sands from where a quirky sea tractor (like the one at Burgh Island) transports people out to a ferry that runs to the main town during the summer months. However if you have had enough of water-based fun for one day, it's just a final calf-stretching climb up a small hill and back down to North Sands and the starting point. It's then got to be time to reward yourself with a well-deserved ice cream from the famous Salcombe Dairy, or perhaps a warming tipple in the Winking Prawn during the colder winter months.

DIRECTIONS

1 The walk begins at North Sands car park. Follow the road with the beach on your left as it curves up along Cliff Road, bearing right at the brown sign towards South Sands. Wind up the hill past 'The Moult' and then fork right at the post box to continue along Moult Road. The road becomes a track and continues into the woods. Fork left and cross the stile to head down through the trees to the road.
0.8 miles

2 Turn right and follow the road up to the thatched village of Combe, forking left by the post box and bench to continue up the road to Rew. Just before the brow of the hill, turn left at the public footpath sign for Soar. The path takes you into Higher Rew Caravan and Camping

Park. Continue on the green lane by the barn and then turn right into the field, following the hedges up the hill, before turning right to cross the cattle grid.
0.7 miles

3 Cross over to follow the lane past the rear of the coastguard cottages at Soar, continuing along to the next junction with a grassy bank dropping down to some barn conversions. Ignore the footpath on the left, but instead take the left-hand turn onto the drive signed for Soar Mill Cove. Continue past the thatched cottage at Lower Soar (ignoring another footpath) and follow the road left after the hotel and then through a gate on the right onto the footpath down to Soar Mill Cove.
0.8 miles

4 After your swim, follow the South West Coast Path signed for Salcombe up the hill above the cove, with the sea on your right. The path drops down into a valley and back up the other side, before flattening out along the Warren. Walk through the gap in the hedge and then fork right following the Coast Path around Bolt Head, descending down a steep hill to Starehole Bay.
2 miles

5 Cross a bridge and up the steps to round the dramatic cliff path at Sharp Tor. Continue though Fir Wood and into the National Trust car park at Overbecks. Continue straight on down the road to South Sands and then past the beach and up the hill before dropping back down to North Sands and the car park where you began.
1.4 miles

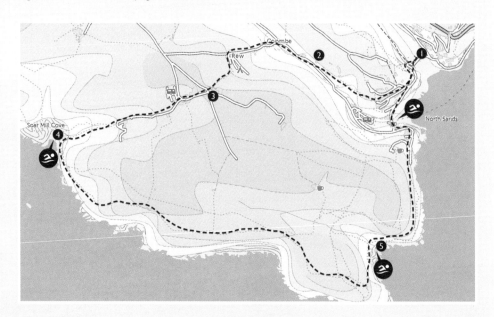

Walk 20

WOODCOMBE SANDS AND IVY COVE CIRCULAR

Gin-clear sea, rocky platforms and unusual raised beaches all feature on this beautiful walk through the remote southernmost point of Devon.

Both the beaches featured on this walk are bristling with channels and gulleys, so you can have a real adventure swimming through mazes of rocks, over beautiful colourful bedrock, and through kelp gardens.

The walk starts in the village of East Prawle ❶, which has acquired something of a cult status due to its rock star connections. The landlord of the pub the Pig's Nose used to be in the music business, and has persuaded star names including Damon Albarn of Blur, and Paul Young, to perform in the hall next to the pub. Sadly though Kate Bush, who has a holiday home nearby, has not yet been persuaded to appear.

There are lots of campsites in the village, mostly very basic in farmers' fields. Many people come down for the entire summer and it is fun to camp for the night after you've done the walk. You could then do our Start Point walk the following day and make a weekend of it (or indeed the other way round!)

As you walk down towards the sea, you will see the promontory of Prawle Point to your right. The word Prawle comes from the Anglo Saxon, meaning 'lookout', and it has served this purpose throughout the centuries, including during the Napoleonic and World Wars. HM Coastguard set it up as a coastguard station after the war, but it was closed during a period of cutbacks. In the 1990s a voluntary organisation, the National Coastwatch Institution, was set up to fill the gap and now teams of volunteer watchkeepers keep a visual watch over the coastline here. There is an interesting visitor centre which is worth a detour if you have time, and the watchkeepers are a friendly bunch.

INFORMATION

DISTANCE: 5 miles
TIME: 2-3 hours
MAP: OS Explorer South Devon OL20
START POINT: East Prawle village green (SX 780 363, TQ7 2BY). Park at the green or on roads in the village
END POINT: East Prawle village green
PUBLIC TRANSPORT: The Coleridge community bus; check website for details: coleridgebus. co.uk
SWIMMING: Woodcombe Cove (SX 796 368), Ivy Cove (SX 799 369)
PLACES OF INTEREST: Prawle Point Coastwatch, Ivy Cove
REFRESHMENTS: The Pig's Nose Inn, an eccentric pub, always very busy, with good food and real ales, and baskets of knitting for you to do if you're that way inclined! Don't try and pay with a card as they only take cash or cheques (01548 511209, TQ7 2BY). The Piglet Café, East Prawle is a lovely, friendly café serving up great breakfasts and cream teas (01548 511486, TQ7 2BY)

As you get down onto the coast path, you get an incredible view of Prawle Point, the 'horse's head'. It is very striking, but also infuriating as you can't get a decent photograph as you're so far away! The only way to get closer to it is in a boat. Don't, whatever you do, swim anywhere near Prawle Point, as the currents around it are really dangerous.

Down on the coast path, as you head east towards Start Point, you'll notice wheat fields, with rocky cliffs behind them. This land formation is unusual and very exciting to geologists. The cliffs behind the fields mark the old coastline, before a major period of geological change. They are formed of hornblende schist, and have a beautiful green tint. The 'raised beach', or 'wave-cut platform', which forms the coastline today was created around ten thousand years ago, towards the end of the last ice age, when sea levels were about seven metres higher than they are today, as a result of the ice sheets melting. At the same time, mud was pouring over the cliffs and settling on the flat strip of land that was left behind when the sea level dropped again, creating a fertile platform, which started to be farmed in the Bronze Age. Until fairly recently cauliflowers were farmed here, with the farmers using seaweed from the beaches as fertiliser, but at the moment wheat seems to be the crop of choice.

Continuing along the coast path, look out for birds of prey soaring above the cliffs to your left. If you're lucky you might see a peregrine falcon, but buzzards and kestrels are more likely. Look out for cirl bunting too; they can often be seen on top of the hedges, alongside yellowhammers and stonechats. Another rarity to be seen around here is the delicate pearl-bordered fritillary butterfly.

You'll pass Maelcombe House, formerly

an Edwardian mansion, which has now been demolished and is being rebuilt as a new luxury home. Local rumour has it that the new owner is a millionaire from Wales, who invented a widget which is in every single mobile phone sold throughout the world. There are lots of pretty flowers around the path here, including some roses growing down the cliff: escapees from the long-established garden. It's a house in splendid isolation and with impressive views.

You pass Horseley Cove, which is a long, wild beach but only good for swimming at high tide due to the rocky shelf. It's best to head for Woodcombe Sand ❹ a truly idyllic beach, with incredibly clear water. A seemingly unused boathouse is the only sign of human presence. The bay has a beautiful bedrock of grey and white striped stone, which is stunning to swim over. There are platforms on the left hand side of the beach (looking at the sea) that you can dive off at high water (always check the depth first), as well as channels and inlets to explore. There are a couple

of islands to the right of the beach called Ballsaddle Rock, where there are lots of cormorants and other sea birds.

Ivy Cove ❺, the next beach, is only 10 minutes walk from Woodcombe. You can swim between the two if you want. Until 40 years ago there was a small fishing fleet based in the cove, and it was a real working place, unlike today. The rusty old winch the fishermen used is still there. Sophie's dad went on holiday there as a boy, in 1938, and stayed with a fishing family, the Logans, who lived in the cottages above the beach. Amazingly, Bill Logan, a descendant of the family, still lives in the cottages.

In 1938 the beach was a hive of activity. The fishermen went mainly for crabs and lobster, and you can still see the iron rings in the rocks where pots and boats were anchored. Life was tough and there weren't many luxuries. Sophie's father Roger remembers how all the rubbish would get tipped out from the cottages directly down the cliff, which was consequently alive

with rats. He and his brother would amuse themselves by hiding under the tarpaulin covering the boats and shooting the rats with an air gun.

Bill Logan, the last descendant of the fishermen from the cove, tells us that the fishing stopped here when the family switched to larger, motor-powered boats, and started fishing out of Dartmouth. It is lovely that he is still there, a permanent resident with his beautifully tended garden and vegetable patch by the sea. It will probably become yet another holiday cottage when he dies.

Swimming at Ivy Cove is wonderful. You can swim along to the next beach, Lannacombe, over forests of kelp and maiden's tresses seaweed, exploring a maze of channels, and sheltered from the main body of the sea by numerous large rocks. There are several lagoons where many local youngsters learned to swim in the past.

Ivy Cove is a bit of a well-kept secret; it is not marked on the Ordnance Survey map, and there was a huge cliff fall in January 2013 which resulted in the cliff path being diverted, which has taken walkers away from the beach. So enjoy the sense of isolation and let your mind wander back to when it was a much busier place.

The walk takes you back up through a pretty wood and through the fields to the village, where you can have a well-earned pint in the Pig's Nose pub. Not only that, but it offers free wine gums and snuff, and 'stress therapy with barmaids'! If you have more time in the area then it's also worth exploring west along the coast path to the wonderful sandy swimming coves of Elender (best in the morning as it's east-facing) and Venerick 's (known locally as Moor Sands).

DIRECTIONS

1 From the village green, take the road south towards the sea, going past Mollie Tucker's field on the left. Follow the road downhill past Ash Park on the right, ignoring the public bridleway sign. Stay on the road and go past the Little Holloway campsite on the left.
0.5 miles

2 You will see a sign pointing left saying Public Footpath, Link to Coast Path. Turn left here and walk through the field towards the next field, with the hedge on your left. Walk past an old bath (serving as a trough!) and continue to the bottom of the hill.
0.2 miles

3 Go through the left hand stile and turn left, picking up the coast path. You are now walking east. Follow the coast path past Maelcombe House (at the time of writing, the house was being rebuilt). Keep following the path up and around a rocky headland (getting uneven underfoot) until you come to a signpost pointing right to Woodcombe Sands.
1.7 miles

4 Turn right here to go down to the beach. Coming back from the beach, re-join the coast path eastwards. Ignore a left hand sign for Woodcombe, and keep following the coast path. Ignore the sign for Lannacombe, and go straight on where the sign says Public Footpath, Ivy Cove (Dead End). Follow the path past the terrace of three cottages on the left and down to the beach.

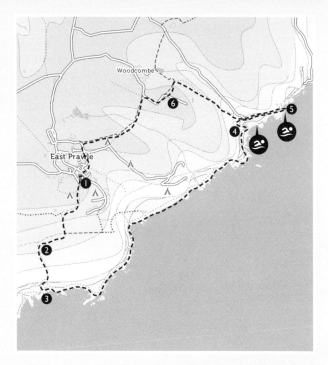

0.5 miles

5 Coming back, retrace your steps until the sign for Woodcombe, turn right here and ascend through the wood. The path emerges onto a track. Keep going up the hill and through a five-bar gate, and continue to follow the path between two hedges. Turn left where a sign says Public Bridleway.
0.8 miles

6 You then reach a five-bar gate and turn right into the road. Keep walking and you will see a small sign with a blue arrow on it pointing right. Follow the road to the right

here. Then turn left where there is a sign saying Public Bridleway, East Prawle ½ mile. Follow the path with a cornfield on your left, down into a wood and up again. The path bears right and you then turn left where there is a sign saying Public Bridleway. This takes you back to the village.
0.9 miles

Walk 21

START POINT CIRCULAR

A wonderful wild adventure past a Gothic lighthouse and across a dramatic headland, before dropping down to swim at a secret beach.

INFORMATION

DISTANCE: 2 miles
TIME: 2-3 hours
MAP: OS Explorer South Devon OL20
START POINT: Start Point car park (SX 820 375, TQ7 2ET)
END POINT: Start Point car park
PUBLIC TRANSPORT: The number 3 bus between Dartmouth and Plymouth stops at Stokenham, from where you would need to get a taxi to the start
SWIMMING: The hidden beach at Peartree Point (SX 819 366), and Great Mattiscombe Sands (SX 816 369).
PLACES OF INTEREST: Start Point Lighthouse.
REFRESHMENTS: The Start Bay Inn at Torcross is a thatched pub dating back to the 14th century, serving famous fish and chips and seafood specialities with stunning views across Slapton Sands and the bay (01548 580553, TQ7 2TQ). The Millbrook Inn at South Pool is a friendly and fun hostelry serving delicious pub grub and with a 24-hour produce shop operated on an honesty system (01548 531581, TQ7 2RW)

The car park at Start Point must be a contender for one of the best views of any car park in the UK, with views back across to Beesands and the ruins at Hallsands to your left, and down to the lighthouse to your right. The walk down to the lighthouse is like walking over the spiny tail of some gargantuan prehistoric beast, and indeed the name 'start' derives from the Anglo-Saxon term 'steort' meaning 'tail'. The dramatic gothic-style lighthouse ❷ was built back in 1836 on what is one of the most rugged and exposed peninsulas in the UK, running almost a mile into the sea. Designed by James Walker (who designed 29 lighthouses including the Needles, Wolf Rock and Bishop Rock), the contractor Hugh McIntosh was actually blind, but this didn't stop him supervising the build of this impressive structure.

It's definitely worth taking the 45 minute tour to discover the fascinating history of what is the only working lighthouse open to the public in Devon. It was the first lighthouse in the UK to be fitted with Alan Stevenson's revolutionary dioptric apparatus, a refractive lens using prisms rather than the traditional silver mirrors. Incredibly the system works so well that the beam of light slicing through the darkness only uses a 1000 watt bulb. Before electrification, oil burners would have used herring oil, sperm whale oil, seal oil and rape seed oil to power the light. An eerie sounding bell was introduced in the 1860s for use in heavy fog, followed in 1876 by an equally unnerving fog horn that can be heard as far away as Salcombe.

With all this equipment, three lighthouse keepers and their families were based at Start Point, in dwellings that can now be rented as holiday accommodation. They were as self-sufficient as possible, with vegetable gardens, a pigsty and chicken coops. A steep path led down the cliff to a beach where they were able to launch a fishing boat, while they would also catch rabbits and collect seagull eggs. The lighthouse was automated in 1993.

Continuing over the dragon's back, the path takes a dramatic turn as it winds its way around the vertiginous contours of the coast, dropping right down to exposed cliff edges with sharp drops to rocky bays and gullies below. This wild exposed section of the walk is truly spectacular, and on a clear day you can see the horse head shape of the natural arch at Prawle Point in the distance. This is another extremely hazardous stretch of coast for ships, and back in 1873 the tea clipper Lalla Rookh struck the rocks here and disgorged all 1,300 tons of cargo. Apparently the tea formed a bank 10 feet high, which was quarried away by the wives of the fisherman living there. It would seem that not only was salt in their blood, but in their tea as well.

As the path drops down closer to the sea at Peartree Point ❸, you can reach a secret shingle beach surrounded by several rocky islands. It's a delightful spot for a dip, although stay close to the coast, as there are some strong currents out near the islands. A natural channel between sea cliffs and the rocky islands guides you out into the azure waters of a lagoon, with the lighthouse standing as a guardian in the distance. Swim off to the left and you'll discover a cave to explore, while there are also several tempting rocks to jump from. The area is also home to a grey seal

colony, although don't worry, as they seemed more scared of us when we visited. There are also several underwater arches here, which probably make for a perfect play and hunting ground for these curious mammals.

You get great views over Great Mattiscombe Beach ❹ as you walk around the headland. The curious geology makes the spot popular for students, with a raised beach and natural conical pillars resembling the chimneys of a tin mine. The raised beach reflects the sea level millions of years ago. It is covered in glacial debris from the last ice age and the conical pillars are the remains that haven't yet been eroded away. We think the double-layered beach looks a bit like the circle and stalls at a theatre, looking over the striking Great Rock, which seems precariously balanced at low tide when it is fully exposed.

The beach was once known as 'More Rope Bay,' thanks to a rather wretched local legend. When a ship was lured onto the rocks by wreckers looking to plunder the cargo, some more upstanding local

villagers attempted to rescue the crew from the rocks where they were stranded. They lowered a rope down the cliffs but it wasn't long enough. The survivors desperately called for more rope as the tide rose around them. The beach at Great Mattiscombe Sands was also used as a filming location in Tim Burton's comedy vampire fantasy, Dark Shadows starring Johnny Depp, albeit with towering CGI cliffs that were added in later.

Set up base on the beach and prepare for some delicious swimming in these sparkling waters. When we arrived a group of lads were making full use of the first rock as a natural diving platform, while we entered the water near the Great Rock and swam off to the right. This area of the beach is popular for bouldering (low level climbing without ropes) and we headed off in the direction of the conical pillars, which one wit in our party compared to Madonna's Jean Paul Gaultier bra. It was mid-tide and we passed plenty of rocks to conquer and jump from, before swimming through a natural maze of channels and then back towards the dark golden sands, to bake dry in the sunshine.

It's a much shorter walk back up to the car park through some beautiful fields. Keep an eye out for some colourful butterflies including green hair-streaks and clouded yellows, while in the spring and summer you may be fortunate to spot a cirl bunting, as well as ravens and buzzards hovering on the air currents above potential prey. We combined this swim walk with a night camping in Sally Tripp's field at East Prawle, with stunning views down to the sea. It was then off for a few ales in the legendary Pigs Nose Inn, where we reminisced about the day's adventurers, before a final warming nightcap at the campsite under a magnificent blanket of stars.

DIRECTIONS

1 The walk begins in the pay car park at Start Point, which is worth every penny for the incredible views alone. Head out through the gate or over the stile and follow the Coast Path down the old lighthouse road towards the sea, until you reach the lighthouse.
0.6 miles

2 After visiting the lighthouse, continue to follow the coast path west along the cliffs until you reach the small headland of Peartree Point. Here you can climb down to the secret shingle beach and swim spot. Do stay close to the coast when swimming as there are some strong currents further out near the larger rocky islands.
0.7 miles

3 From Peartree Point, continue to the west along the coast path to Great Mattiscombe Sand, walking down the steps to the beach.
0.3 miles

4 Follow the track uphill from the beach and through several gates to return to the car park half a mile away.
0.4 miles

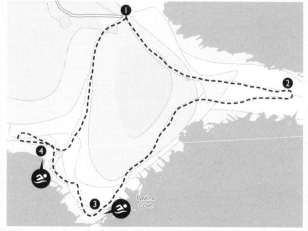

BEESANDS TO HALLSANDS CIRCULAR

This stunning circular coastal walk takes in charming fishing villages, magnificent countryside and a swim to a ruined village.

O
ur walk begins in Beesands, an amiable seaside village with a permanent population of around 100 people and several converted fishermen's cottages, now available as popular holiday lets. Park for free next to Britannia @ the Beach, a seafood shack, waiting to reward you with delicious fish soup and seafood treats on your return. This is the retail outlet of Britannia Fisheries, which provides fish and shellfish to restaurants right across the region. Crab, lobster, bass, mackerel, turbot, skate and lemon sole are often landed at Beesands, as well as diver-caught scallops, mussels, clams and oysters.

Begin your walk with the sea on your left and the striking Start Point Lighthouse in the distance. Several of the fishing cottages you pass have porch seats built into the entrances, which would once have provided views out to sea for wives eagerly awaiting the return of their fishermen husbands. Today the sea defences block some of this view, but not for us upright walkers. When we visited, one of our group described the view (from the Daymark tower above Dartmouth to the left, around to the lighthouse to the right) as a wide-screen cinematic panorama. She pointed out that much of the Devon coast has smaller bays with natural rocky arms to cradle them, while this bay is completely open and exposed.

On your right you'll pass the Cricket Inn, which dates back to 1867 and is another great place to enjoy freshly caught seafood. Its surprising claim to fame is that a pre-Rolling Stones Keith Richards and Mick Jagger played their first ever gig here. Apparently Richards' family regularly spent holidays in the village and one summer they invited an adolescent Mick along, who complained about the lack of young girls in the area. The pair turned to music to fill the void and the rest is history. It's not the

INFORMATION

DISTANCE: 3 miles
TIME: 3 hours
MAP: OS Explorer South Devon OL20
START POINT: Car park at Beesands (SX 819 405, TQ7 2EH)
END POINT: Car park at Beesands
PUBLIC TRANSPORT: Coleridge Community Bus runs to Beesands and North Hallsands from Kingsbridge on Fridays only. Call 01548 580402
SWIMMING: North Hallsands (SX 817 389) to the ruined village and back; the beach at Beesands (SX 819 404)
PLACES OF INTEREST: Beesands, ruined village at Hallsands
REFRESHMENTS: The Cricket Inn is popular with locals and visitors alike, serving seafood including crab, lobster and scallops caught in Start Bay (01548 580215, TQ7 2EN). Britannia @ the Beach (affectionately known as 'The Shack') is a combination of a fishmonger, village store and unique seafood café (01548 581168, TQ7 2EH). Their crab soup is to die for!

only unexpected rock and roll connection we will uncover along the way.

The walk joins the coast path at a thatched cottage and the track soon leads you up to magnificent exposed fields, strewn with bracken. The path will take you around Tinsey Head, which is carpeted with bluebells in the spring and boasts tempting glimpses of sparkling waters below. Looking out across Start Bay, you'll spot the Skerries Bank Bell Buoy, which marks the north eastern end of a notorious shallow shingle bank that has been the cause of countless shipwrecks. The Skerries Bank stretches across to the lighthouse and is legendary for plaice fishing.

Also on the hunt for fish are the guillemots and razorbills you'll see sitting on the polished sea, like surfers waiting for the perfect wave. Every now and again they dive deep into the waters below and the lucky ones will return to the surface with a dark silver prize glinting in their beaks. In the summer months the cliffs are also home to a breeding colony of kittiwakes. You should keep an eye out for kestrels soaring on the wind too, hunting land-based prey. Sightings of basking sharks and dolphins are also common in the bay.

The shingle beach at the small hamlet of North Hallsands (known locally as Greenstraight) is backed by a reed bed and is popular with local fishermen, who inform us they often catch bass, flatfish and plaice from this picturesque spot. It's also popular with pop stars. Blur's Damon Albarn (who has a holiday home nearby) was inspired to write the Gorillaz album Plastic Beach after taking a stroll at North Hallsands and discovering lots of plastic particles washed up between the pebbles. It led to a meditation on the state of our oceans and the discovery that there is a huge expanse of debris floating in the Pacific Ocean. On the album, the

Gorillaz characters exist on the floating rubbish tip.

It is fun and fascinating to swim to the lost village ❸. At low tide you can scramble along the shore but be careful not to get cut off. Alternatively if you walk up towards the coastguard cottages on the headland, there is a viewing platform looking over the ruined village. A detailed information board also shares the wretched tale of how a once-thriving fishing village was condemned by the stupidity of man. A giant dredging operation to supply gravel for the building of the naval dockyard at Devonport saw half a million tons of shingle removed from the Skerries Bank. The massive operation caused the beach level to drop by four metres, leaving the village exposed to high tides and easterly winds. Several buildings were destroyed or damaged during storms in 1903 and 1904, and urgent action was taken, including the building of a new sea wall. However a major storm in 1917 caused further destruction and the village was abandoned. All in all, the dredging ultimately caused 37 houses to slip into the sea. The information board includes a poignant poem by John Masefield:

"But that its wretched ruins then
though sunken utterly
will show the brute greed of men
helps feed the greedy sea."

Swimming to the ruins is unforgettable. You head south from the beach, with the coast on your right, passing Wilson's Rock. The village is a melancholy site, with the remains of houses hanging off the cliff; amazingly you can still see bits of furniture. It's incredible to think that in the 1800s, the village was home to 159 people. There was a pub called the London Inn with

stables and a piggery, a shop with a post office, a grocery, a community centre and even allotments. Nearly all the men in the village made their living from fishing, with women and children posted on the clifftops looking out for shoals of fish. Fishing boats were stored on the beach and, in really rough conditions, Newfoundland dogs were trained to swim out into the waves and return with the boats' ropes clenched between their teeth.

When you are ready to continue the walk, head up the steps towards Prospect House ❸ (also known as Trout's Apartments), which resembles something from the New England Coast and hides a remarkable history. It was originally built by two tenacious sisters who had lost their homes and livelihood when the village was destroyed. With a compensation payment they bought a plot of land, and then with a loan the plucky pair employed an out-of-work blacksmith to make bricks from the shingle on the beach. They used the 8,000 bricks to build a small guest house with their bare hands. This developed into the Trout's Hotel, which thrived for 30 years before being extended into the coastal apartments you see today.

It's a really pleasant walk back through the several ancient green lanes dating back centuries. It's incredible to think that people may have been travelling along these same routes as far back as the Bronze Age some 4,000 years ago. Look out for the willow growing by the stream, which would have provided the materials for making crab pots. It's then a genuinely spectacular walk down the side of fields and back to your starting point, where refreshments in the inn or seafood shack must be on the cards.

DIRECTIONS

❶ Park for free by Britannia @ the Beach in Beesands. Walk to the right (with the sea on your left) and follow the coast defences past cottages and the Cricket Inn. At the sign saying No parking turning beyond this point, turn right past the thatch cottage and follow the sign saying Hallsands 1m.
0.1 miles

❷ Once out of the village and on the coast path, follow it through several gates and finally down onto the beach at Hallsands. Walk to the end of the beach and if you are wanting to swim to the ruined village, change into swim gear near the slipway.
0.7 miles

❸ To view the ruined village from the shore, take the road to the southern end of the village and climb a long flight of steps, until you reach Prospect House/ Trout's Apartments. Bear right down the road and then after about 150 metres turn right opposite Trout's Car Park and climb over the stile onto the public footpath. You will see the viewing platform ahead. After admiring the ruins below, return to the main beach.
0.3 miles

❹ Go back to the northern end of the beach, turning left after the gate. Continue along the path, passing a pond on the left before bearing right into a green lane.
0.4 miles

❺ After about 200 metres and by a small stream, turn right onto a track which becomes another green lane. After you reach Higher Middlecombe Farm, bear right up the green lane to follow the red waymarker. When you meet the surfaced road, turn right and then after about 100 metres turn right again to follow a green waymarker for Beesands.
0.5 miles

❻ Follow the fields down towards the sea and then turn left following the waymarker. When you reach the coast path, turn left and retrace your steps back to Beesands.
0.8 miles

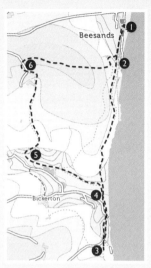

Walk 23

LITTLE DARTMOUTH, COMPASS COVE, SUGARY COVE, CASTLE COVE CIRCULAR

A glorious coastal walk with spectacular views. It takes in meadows, pasture and woods, culminating in a thrilling swim through a high sided chasm linking Sugary and Castle Coves.

INFORMATION

DISTANCE: 3 miles
TIME: 3 hours
TIDES: If you wish to swim through the chasm at Sugary Cove, you need to time your walk to coincide roughly with high water – give or take an hour either side. You need to allow an hour from the start of the walk to get to Sugary Cove.
MAP: OS Explorer South Devon OL20
START POINT: Little Dartmouth car park (SX 874 491, TQ6 0JR)
END POINT: Little Dartmouth car park
PUBLIC TRANSPORT: Buses to Dartmouth from Plymouth and Brixham. Steam train from Paignton to Dartmouth
SWIMMING: Compass Cove SX 884 494, Sugary Cove SX 885 501, Castle Cove SX 886 502
PLACES OF INTEREST: Dartmouth Castle
REFRESHMENTS: The Castle Tea Rooms by Castle Cove, is a charming café overlooking the castle and estuary serving locally caught crab, as well as cream teas (01803 833897, TQ6 0JN). There are plenty of pubs and restaurants in Dartmouth itself, including 'Alf's' - Café Alf Resco – a bit of a Dartmouth institution, renowned for its breakfasts and friendly atmosphere (01803 835880, TQ6 9AN)

The minute you start this walk you are assailed by stunning views to every side. Walking down towards the coast path you can see the famous Daymark in the distance on your left. It is a huge octagonal stone tower which was built in 1864 to guide mariners in to Dartmouth. It is visible for miles, including from Dartmoor. Meanwhile on your right, you can see all the way down to Start Point with great views of the long shingle beach at Slapton Sands.

As you walk, especially if it's a lovely summer's day, you'll quickly become aware of what a busy place Dartmouth is for mariners. Nearer towards the mouth of the estuary, you'll see all manner of boats out and about, from the little white sails of dinghies, through to fishing and pleasure boats, and the odd cargo ship further out to sea.

There are usually cattle grazing in the fields above the coast, including an unusual herd of British Whites, one of the oldest breeds in Britain. They are white, with black ears and noses. They are very gentle and are unusual in that when they have calves, they take it in turn to watch over them while the rest of the herd grazes. Also, look out for linnets, stonechats and yellowhammers which can often be seen.

You may notice some small islands out to sea. The smaller, nearer one is the Western Blackstone. Further out and larger is the Mewstone. The walk then takes you down a picturesque valley, with a triple fingerpost at the bottom. This is where you can head off to Compass Cove ❺ if you wish to. This is a lovely little beach with

a cave and lots of rocks for climbing. It has some unusual orange pebbles. It is quite a sun trap and a great place to hang out for an hour or two - and enjoy a dip of course!

There is more to this beach than meets the eye though. It contains the ruins of an old Victorian cable house, which was used to pioneer an early form of communication. In 1884 an undersea telegraph cable was laid to Guernsey. It was 92 miles long, and electric signals were transmitted over wires to send messages. It was in use until the 1950s, except during the German occupation of the Channel Islands in World War Two, when it was severed.

Further on from Compass Cove is Blackstone Point **6**, where there is a raised beach, consisting of a series of rocky ledges, where many people like to fish. This is also a great place to swim from when it is calm, as the water is incredibly clear. However the main swimming destination is Sugary Cove **8**, the next stop on the walk. You descend through attractive woods which are full of bluebells in May, to find a small beach bordered by angular slate cliffs.

It is best to visit the beach at high tide, so as to get the most exciting swim. Head out into the bay, keeping to your left. Keep looking to your left, and you will see a gap in the rocks. This leads into a spectacular channel, linking through to Castle Cove next door. We call it the 'Ravine'. Swimming through here is an amazing experience, although do not attempt it if the sea is rough. The rocks tower up either side of you, and there is a small oak tree leaning overhead. The play of light on the rock walls is entrancing, and when the water is calm and clear you may see fish, spider crabs and starfish. You emerge at Castle Cove where the dramatic atmosphere continues, as the castle overshadows the scene. Slightly more prosaic is the sign on the

rocks below the castle, warning of the danger of the rising tide!

This sign – along with one reading '6 knots' is on a concrete platform just below the castle, which dates from Victorian times. Castle Cove was, and still is, the town's main beach, but is small and virtually disappears at high water. So the towns-people decided to create a bathing platform on the rocks, and connected it via a bridge to the little beach, so it was accessible at all states of the tide. Sadly now the connection to the bridge from the beach has been washed away, but it is still fun to swim to the platform, and it is a great place to dive and jump from at high water.

If you have non-swimmers with you they can bring your stuff along to Castle Cove and meet you there, or else it is just as easy, and probably more enjoyable, to swim back the way you came and enjoy seeing it all again from a different angle. We often get close up to sea birds here, as they like to perch on the rocks and don't seem to notice you when you're in the water – if you're quiet. Oyster catchers are particularly common, and are a beautiful sight with their bright orange bills and legs. It is really interesting to stop and observe these birds at such close quarters.

Dartmouth Castle is well worth a visit. Construction was started in 1388 to defend the port, and it contains numerous exciting guns, cannons and the like. It has an amazing position, built right on top of the rocks, almost overhanging the water, and incorporates the ancient church of St Petrox. It was fought over by the Royalists and the Parliamentarians in the English Civil War, and also played a role in the First and Second World Wars.

The walk finishes by taking you inland, through a farm, but the amazing views continue as you are still high up.

DIRECTIONS

1 From the car park walk south along the track with the sea ahead of you.
0.4 miles

2 At the stile turn left and walk east with the sea on your right.
0.3 miles

3 Turn left through the gap in the stone wall and continue with the sea on your right. You're now walking north, towards Dartmouth.
0.1 miles

4 After an ascent you reach a fork in the path – take the right hand fork. This path takes you down a picturesque valley.
0.5 miles

5 At the bottom you will see a sign to Compass Cove on the right. If you wish to visit it, go off here, and then return to the main path and follow it with the sea on your right.
0.2 miles

6 At the next headland, which is called Blackstone Point, you can do another diversion by climbing through a hole in the hedge and going onto some rocky ledges below which are fun to swim off on a calm day. Otherwise follow the path which starts to ascend through woods.
0.4 miles

7 You reach a fingerpost with a bird box on top, with Compass Cottage on the left. Just past the fingerpost there is a path on the right down to Sugary Cove.
0.1 miles

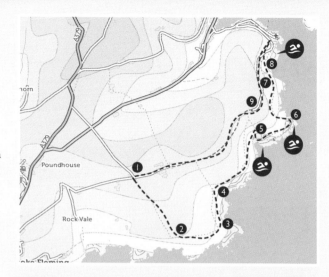

8 Leaving Sugary Cove, do not take the same path back up as it is very steep. Instead, take the other footpath up from the beach and bear right; this will bring you out on Sugary Green and the road. If you wish to visit the castle, follow the footpath off to the right of the road which takes you down to the castle. Afterwards retrace your steps and follow the lane back to Compass Cottage where you take the right hand fork.
0.2 miles

9 You reach a gate with a sign saying Private, Coastguard Rescue, Police and Emergency Vehicles Only. Go through here, and through the stile into land with the National Trust Little Dartmouth sign. Head through the farm, following the Public Bridleway to NT car park sign, which takes you back to the car park.
1 mile

Walk 24

MILL BAY CIRCULAR

An energetic walk through rolling farmland with spectacular clifftops and headlands, taking in some remarkable military history and a swim from a secluded beach.

O ur walk starts in one of the two National Trust parks near their Coleton Fishacre property, which is well worth visiting either before or after your mini-adventure. It was the home of Rupert and Lady Dorothy D'Oyly Carte. Built in the Arts and Crafts style, it has extravagant Art Deco interiors and a garden full of exotic plants. The property runs right down to the sea, where there is a small seawater pool (sadly no longer accessible by foot), which was no doubt the location of several Jazz Age shindigs. The music of Gilbert and Sullivan would also have been prevalent, as Rupert's father Richard was the impresario behind their operettas. When he wasn't building on his father's legacy, expanding his hotels like the Savoy and revitalising Gilbert and Sullivan productions, he enjoyed fast cars. Indeed he was once fined £3 for driving 19 miles an hour in 1902. He also enjoyed yachting and chose to build a property on this stretch of coast after sailing past, correctly believing it to be one of the most beautiful in the world.

The walk takes you down past some stunning National Trust properties which are available to rent, including Higher Brownstone Farm and Crockers Cottage. Look out for a rookery in the tree just below the farm. A gate takes you from the farm track and onto an ancient lane where centuries of hooves and feet have worn the land away to create a holloway ❸, with the bedrock exposed beneath. The shady bucolic track passes pretty woods and a bubbling stream over the low wall to the left, carpeted with the yellow of Wordsworth's favourite wild flower, the lesser celandine, every spring. Crossing the bridge over the brook you'll pass some

INFORMATION

DISTANCE: 3 miles
TIME: 2-3 hours
MAP: OS Explorer South Devon OL20
START POINT: Higher Brownstone car park (SX 904 509, TQ6 0EH)
END POINT: Higher Brownstone car park
PUBLIC TRANSPORT: Kingswear can be reached by steam train from Paignton, or by ferry from Dartmouth. Buses include the 18 bus from Brixham, the 120 bus from Paignton. The main buses to Dartmouth are the 3 from Plymouth and the X64 from Exeter
SWIMMING: Mill Bay Cove (SX 893 504)
PLACES OF INTEREST: Coleton Fishacre, Mill Bay Cove, Brownstone Battery, The Daymark
REFRESHMENTS: The 15th century Ship Inn in Kingswear has great views of the River Dart from its terrace (01803 752348, TQ6 0AG). There is a nice café with lots of outdoor space at Coleton Fishacre. They are also happy for you to eat your own packed lunch at their picnic tables (01803 842382, TQ6 0EQ).

this section of the coast path is dedicated to his memory. The walk continues down the wooden steps and through Warren Woods to the beach and a castle-like structure ❺. Originally a lime kiln built in the early 19th century, it was later converted into a boathouse and watermill. The parapet and turret with their battlements and the arched Gothic doorway were added towards the end of the century, to make the structure resemble a castle. It certainly adds a touch of the Famous Five to the swim.

If you are here at low tide, the shingle gives way to sand and you'll find yourself in rock pool heaven. At a higher tide, you'll be able to swim out a short way and then off to the right to discover an impressive cave, the height of at least two buses, which you can swim through. This takes you around a corner and back out through another entrance, depositing you a surprising distance from where you started. Swim around the rocks and back towards the shore, or cross to the other side of the bay to discover a secret lagoon. It's an idyllic little spot to float around in circles watching the boats arriving or leaving the mouth of the estuary, or looking up to the pines above the millionaire mansion of Warren House, where our energetic journey will continue.

It's certainly a robust ascent up to The Warren ❻, but you are rewarded with a scented nature reserve of Monterey and Corsican pines, with their needles forming a soft path underfoot. You'll spot lots of these trees along this stretch of coast, which are surprisingly tolerant of the harsh salty sea winds which can batter them during the winter months. You'll walk around the edge of Newfoundland Cove, named after local explorer Humphrey Gilbert who colonised the Canadian province. In the past a fleet of up to 150 vessels would sail from Dartmouth to the fishing grounds

picturesque cottages, as well as a plough and a traditional red phone box. You are entering one of the most desirable addresses in the south west, with some impressive properties to match.

As you turn from the lane to begin the descent to Mill Bay you'll pass a memorial to Lieutenant Colonel Herbert Jones ❹, the former commanding officer of 2nd Battalion Parachute Regiment, who was killed in action during the Battle of Goose Green in the Falklands War. He was posthumously awarded the Victoria Cross and

of Newfoundland at the start of each season, and return with a valuable catch of cod that had been salted and dried from the transatlantic voyage home. The catch would then be exchanged for wine and other luxury goods. The views from here are truly spectacular back down to Mill Bay Cove and Dartmouth Castle, across the mouth of the river. Keep an eye out for falcons, swooping at speeds of up to 200 miles an hour to catch their prey. Other rare birds that can be spotted along this stretch of coast include skylarks, linnets and cirl bunting.

Eventually you will reach the clearing at Inner Froward Point and Brownstone Battery ❼. It's common to spot wild ponies here, which the National Trust use to keep down the scrub and encourage maritime plants and butterflies to flourish. The gun battery was one of several built along the south coast in 1942, as a defence against German U-boats. Brownstone Battery was armed with two six-inch guns recycled from a First World War battleship, with a range of over 14 miles. At night a powerful search light would light up the water below, looking for enemy ships. It seems incredible now that the battery was once manned by up to 300 soldiers, with the cliffs below strung with razor-sharp barbed wire.

The National Coastwatch Institution also have a station at the site. They are a voluntary organisation and registered charity who provide a visual watch along the UK's coast and welcome visitors, so do pop in and say Hi. Their twin duties are to keep a watch over the local coastal area (from Start Point in the west to Brixham in the east), as well as the coast path itself. As you can imagine, this stretch of water near the mouth of the Dart is incredibly busy and the NCI Froward Point alerts Falmouth Coastguard to potential incidents and those in progress. From the lookout there are fantastic views across to the Mewstone, named because it is a nesting site for seabirds including gulls – otherwise known as mews. The rocky island is also the most easterly 'haul-out' for grey seals in the English Channel. The keepers keep a record of seal sighting, as well as marine mammals and sea birds for the relevant wildlife organisations.

It's a bit of a slope back up to the car park, but take a breather to visit the towering eight-legged Daymark ❽, resembling something from the cover of a 1970s concept album. The remarkable structure, the height of two Olympic-sized diving boards was built in the 19th century by the Dartmouth Harbour Commissioners as a day beacon (a sort of daytime lighthouse) to help guide mariners to the entrance of Dartmouth Harbour. Built on such a high exposed plane, the views from here are magnificent and this other-worldly tower, just a short stroll from the car park, makes the perfect finish to this picturesque swim walk adventure.

1 Walk out of the car park and turn left onto the lane and follow it down the gentle slope. Take the right hand fork following the public footpath signposted Kingswear.
0.3 miles

2 Walk past Higher Brownstone Farm on your right and continue down the farm track past the yellow farm cottages. Go through the gate on the left and onto an ancient holloway.
0.1 miles

3 Continue down the sunken lane, which can be quite wet and slippery, and cross a small bridge over a stream and past some quaint cottages and a red phone box. Follow the lane around to the left, pausing to take a photo down the valley to where you can see our swim stop at Mill Bay Cove with its small castle-like structure.
0.4 miles

4 At the end of the lane turn left, following the sign for Froward Point, and past the memorial for Lt. Col. Herbert Jones. Walk down the steps through the wood, and turn right at the bottom and through the gate to Mill Bay.
0.1 miles

5 After your swim, head back through the gate, over the bridge and right on to the track before ascending the steep steps up the hill.
0.1 miles

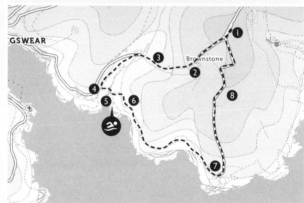

6 At the top, the path winds its way through the pinewoods, before levelling out and revealing stunning views over to the mouth of the estuary and Start Bay beyond. Follow it up and down until you reach the clearing at Inner Froward Point and the remains of the World War II battery.
0.7 miles

7 From the battery, walk up the steep lane following signs for Brownstone car park.
0.4 miles

8 You will reach the iconic Daymark on your right, which is well worth crossing the field to visit. Then return back onto the lane and up to the car park where you began.
0.6 miles

177

Walk 25

MAN SANDS AND SCABBACOMBE CIRCULAR

A short but energetic walk up and down a rollercoaster section of coastal path, visiting two beautiful and secluded beaches, perfect for a refreshing dip.

A sign saying Warning Steep and Uneven Path heralds the start of a picturesque walk down through a valley between lush green rolling hills to the beckoning V of blue sea in the distance. The valley is a beautiful and deceptively relaxing start to an often thigh-straining walk as you head down through two fields to the remote beach at Scabbacombe Sands ❷. As most people don't walk more than ten minutes from where they have parked their cars, and this is a good half hour from the car park, you might well have the sand and pebble beach to yourself. That said, it's popular with naturists and nudist bathers in the summer months, so who knows who you might stumble across!

It's a beautiful spot with wildflowers strewn across the grassy cliffs that plummet right down to the sea, colonised by fulmars, an ocean-going bird resembling a gull. The beach is often a treasure trove of washed-up driftwood and perfect skimming stones, while at low tide you can walk right along to Long Sands, the next beach north. Look out for some amazing geology along the way, including slate formations sculpted by the sea to resemble grey waves. It's a lovely spot for a dip, although do swim close to the shore as there are some really strong currents here, while there are also some submerged rocks off to the left. And don't forget to save a bit of energy, as you'll soon be walking up over that steep cliff in the direction of Brixham.

A brief climb followed by a short drop lulls you into a false sense of security, before the punishing ascent begins. Don't forget to take regular breathers to enjoy the views back towards the ever-shrinking beach and Scabbacombe Head behind it, and then down onto the curve of Long Sands below. If you are visiting between

INFORMATION

DISTANCE: 2.5 miles
TIME: 2-3 hours
MAP: OS Explorer South Devon OL20
START POINT: Car park at Scabbacombe Lane, north east of Kingswear (SX 911 522, TQ6 0EF)
END POINT: Car park at Scabbacombe Lane
PUBLIC TRANSPORT: Bus service 22 and 24 to Hillhead from Brixham and Kingswear and then walk down to the car park
SWIMMING: Scabbacombe Sands (SX 919 519) and Man Sands (SX 923 534)
PLACES OF INTEREST: Man Sands wetlands, Woodhuish Farm
REFRESHMENTS: None on the walk. The nearest café is at the nearby National Trust property, Coleton Fishacre. They are also happy for you to eat your own packed lunch at their picnic tables (01803 752466, TQ6 0EQ). Or visit nearby Brixham where a fishing family has set up a café right by the town's famous lido, with wonderful views: Shoals Café on the Lido (01803 854874, TQ5 9AE).

April and June, look out for early purple orchids and the white star-shaped greater stitchwort in amongst the gorse, ferns and heather, while during the summer months, the area is blanketed with daisies and tall thistle-like teasels with their rosy-purple heads. The path flattens out for about a mile as you head towards Crabrock Point, where it's possible to walk out onto the headland to enjoy stunning views out towards Sharkham Point on the edge of Brixham.

The path now drops down to Man Sands ❸ and the three coastguard cottages, which were built by Napoleonic prisoners of war. Two of the cottages (Crabrock and Ladycove) are available to rent. The cottages date back to the beginning of the 19th century when they provided accommodation for the coastguards, whose primary purpose at that time was looking out for smugglers. Rounding the corner to the beach you'll also spot an old lime kiln and the remains of an old boathouse, which were also built by the prisoners. The kiln was used to make lime to be used as a fertiliser by local farmers.

The pebble and shingle beach becomes exposed sand at a low tide, while a walk off to the right reveals rock pools and a wonderful cave to explore. Return at a higher tide and you can even swim through it if you dare, or perhaps even swim around to the next beach at Short Sands. In the cliffs the more observant might spot a small hole carved into the rock face, just big enough to conceal a person. We've heard it described as a lookout used by the coastguard to watch for smugglers and indeed a secluded hideout for smugglers to watch for the coastguard. Either way it's an amazing find and certainly hints at the very adventurous history of this beautiful beach.

How Man Sands gained its rather masculine name is unknown, but back in 1986 the skeleton of a man was actually found in the sands. According to the South West Coast Path website (southwestcoastpath.org.uk), workers building the sea wall discovered the grave of a young man, believed to have died in a shipwreck. Before the Reverend Hawker from Cornwall started the practice of giving victims of shipwrecks a proper Christian burial, the bodies were either abandoned on the shoreline or buried just above it.

The beach and the land surrounding it are managed by the National Trust and the wetland lagoon fed by a stream has deliberately been allowed to form on an area which was once reclaimed land used for farming. You can spot lots of ducks and waders here, as well as several special species of migrating birds. Along the route back up towards the car park you'll pass a bird hide, which is the perfect place for looking out across the wetland, with interpretation boards to let you know what to look out for.

The return walk also passes Woodhuish, a former Victorian farm also managed by the Trust. Walk up to the barn where you can see the restored cider press that is used to press apples for the annual Apple Day each October. Indeed you can smell the faint scent of apples in the air, while there is also evidence of the barn owls and bats who inhabit the barn, in the pellets and guano covering the cider press. We can only hope they scrub it down before the festival, unless this adds to the flavour of the scrumpy. On that sobering note, it's just a short stroll back up to the car park, something that your thighs will certainly thank you for.

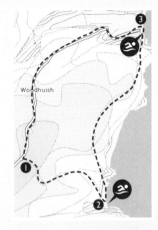

① From the car park at Scabbacombe, walk out through the gate and onto the lane, following the signs for Scabbacombe Sands Link to Coast Path. When you enter the field, follow it around to the left and down the hill before joining the South West Coast Path. Take the path down to the beach for your first potential swim stop.
0.6 miles

② From Scabbacombe Sands, re-join the coast path and follow it back along the coast with the sea on your right. Climb a very steep hill, which flattens out for a mile or so, before dropping down to Man Sands and the second potential swim stop.
1 mile

③ From the beach, head-up Woodhuish Lane, past the cider barn and Woodhuish Farm and back to the car park at the start of Scabbacombe Lane.
1.1 miles

BROADSANDS TO ELBERRY COVE AND CHURSTON COVE CIRCULAR

Ancient woodland, incredible views and fascinating history, this magnificent walk in a spectacular corner of South Devon seems unchanged since Agatha Christie strolled these same paths.

*I*t's worth pausing by the sea wall at Broadsands Beach before you begin this magnificent mini-adventure. Up on the hills overlooking the beach you can see two of Brunel's lofty viaducts, which today carry passengers on the Dartmouth Steam Railway between Paignton and Kingswear. Spin around and you'll take in the traditional beach huts off to your left and then some of the best views in the bay across to Paignton, Torquay and as far as the Dorset coast on a clear day.

The start of the walk takes you past the swanky new pastel-coloured huts (with porches and electricity, don't you know) and then up and around Churston Point. From here you'll be able to see the end of Brixham's half mile long breakwater, a protective arm for this charming fishing port. You'll also spot some black dots on the water in the distance; this is a mussel farm which is run by shellfish producer Brixham Sea Farms. The mussels are a naturally occurring hybrid of the native blue mussel and the Mediterranean mussel. The farm hangs them on ropes where they are left to drift just off the surface of the sea bed until the seed mussels take hold.

The first glimpses of Elberry Cove are a real treat, with its shingle beach spilling into the sparkling turquoise waters. At the far end of the beach you'll spot the remains of Lord Churston's Bathing House ❸, dating back to the 18th century. Lord Churston was the owner of nearby Churston Manor, and a passionate swimmer. The romantic building was originally three storeys, with a ground floor that would flood as the tide came in, so he could swim straight out

INFORMATION

DISTANCE: 3.5 miles
TIME: 4 hours
MAP: OS Explorer South Devon OL20
START POINT: Broadsands car park (SX 897 572, TQ4 6HL)
END POINT: Broadsands car park
PUBLIC TRANSPORT: No 12 Bus from Torquay, Paignton and Brixham
SWIMMING: Elberry Cove (SX 902 570), Churston Cove/ Fishcombe Cove (SX 918 570), Broadsands (SX 896 574)
PLACES OF INTEREST: Lord Churston's Bathing House, lime kilns, Churston Court, Church of St. Mary the Virgin
REFRESHMENTS: There are cafés at Broadsands Beach and Fishcombe Cove – both are seasonal. Churston Court is an historic manor house which is now a hotel and bar (01803 842186, TQ5 0JE). Shoals in nearby Brixham is a café in a beautiful setting by the lido, and has been set up by a local fishing family. Great food and atmosphere (01803 854874, TQ5 9AE)

into the sea through a gated doorway. The designer bathing machine also boasted an early version of a hot tub, with a fire heating up sea water to warm the chilly Lord after his refreshing dip. One of Lord Churston's more famous guests was the future Edward VII, who visited Elberry Cove in 1879 when he was still the Prince of Wales.

It may have been only a quarter of an hour or so since you began the walk, but a swim break here is hard to resist. Avoid the far end of the beach near the bathing house as, incredibly there is a water ski lane here, with boats churning up the water above the eelgrass beds, which are breeding grounds for seahorses. There are also undersea freshwater springs in this area, which can be seen bubbling up through the sea on a calm day. Swim out hugging the coast to the left and you'll be able to enjoy an amazing under-water garden of colourful seaweed and discover sunbathing and jumping rocks. At lower tides this is also a wonderful area for a spot of rock-pooling.

Elberry Cove was a filming location for one of the final scenes in the 1964 film *The System* starring Oliver Reed and directed by Michael Winner. An outrageous beach party takes place here, while scenes were also filmed in the bathing house, which was far more intact at the time. The beach was also a favourite swimming spot of Agatha Christie and indeed the body of Sir Carmichael Clarke was discovered in a field "overlooking the sea and a beach of glistening stones" in *The ABC Murders*.

The steep path from the cove takes you up into Elberry and Marridge Wood, a long narrow stretch of woodland separating the golf course from the sea. You'll catch tantalising glimpses of the sea through these semi-ancient and shady trees, which have been here for over 400 years and include larch

and sweet chestnut. In the spring these woods are carpeted with dog's mercury and drifts of bluebells, while later in the year, the autumnal palette includes the red berries of butcher's broom and the pink fruit of spindle. Several fishermen's paths run off to the left as you walk through this mile and a half stretch of woodland, although be warned, as some paths end in sheer drops down onto the rocks along the stretch of coastline known as Seven Quarries. Much of Torbay's building stone came from these limestone quarries in the 19th century.

The first glimpse of Churston Cove ❹ is spectacular on a sunny day. Boats are often moored just off the shore of this delightful pebbly beach, backed by woodland, giving it a real Mediterranean feel. Before descending, it's worth walking out to the point and taking in the full sweep of the panorama – without doubt one of the best views in the bay. You'll also be able to see the tempting sight of nearby Fishcombe Cove and its small café. A swim between the two coves could be a fun idea, before enjoying a picnic on the

beach and then continuing your adventure. It's widely believed that William of Orange landed his men and artillery here in 1688, before making his renowned landing in Brixham itself.

After you are suitably refreshed, the walk continues up through the woods at the rear of Churston Cove into an area known as The Grove ❺. Within a couple of minutes of entering the woods you'll notice how incredibly quiet and atmospheric this place is. You'll pass through some tree sculptures that were created by an artist called Jack Tree, with the help of local Brixham students. The idea was to create an amphitheatre with carved pillars and tablets overlooked by nine carved faces keeping a watchful eye on the once much-vandalised woodland. Sadly the sculptures have started to decay, but you can still see how beautiful they once were.

You'll also stumble upon a couple of old lime kilns in the woods. Quicklime was an important commodity in the 18th and 19th centuries and it was used to make mortar, plaster and limewash, as well as being added to soil to reduce its acidity. You'll eventually come up out of the woods and along a track with views across to the pretty village

of Churston Ferrers and the sympathetic barn conversions of Churston Court Farm.

Arriving in the village, it's definitely worth a well-earned refreshment break at Churston Court, which has been welcoming people for centuries. The magnificent Grade I listed 12th century manor house is certainly impressive, with large inglenook fires and various rooms to explore, walls covered in original paintings, portraits, tapestries and armour. There are also 17 guest rooms available at this inn, many with four-poster beds. The venue is understandably popular for murder mystery evenings. As you'd expect there's also a ghost: a monk is said to roam the old kitchen.

The former guest list at Churston Court takes in everyone from Sir Humphrey Gilbert (the half-brother of Sir Walter Raleigh, who colonised Newfoundland) to Bruce Reynolds, one of the Great Train Robbers who apparently hid here prior to his arrest in Torquay in 1968. Agatha Christie was also a friend of Lord and Lady Churston and a regular visitor when holidaying at nearby Greenway. She would attend services at the adjacent Church of St. Mary the Virgin ❻, which you will pass as you continue the walk. She even donated the royalties from her Miss Marple short story *Greenshaw's Folly* (which appears in *The Adventure of the Christmas Pudding*) to buy a new east-facing stained glass window for the church in 1955.

The walk continues right through the middle of Churston golf club, which is said to be Christie's inspiration for writing *The Murder on the Links*. You'll then follow a track down past fields of horses and with more magnificent views, finally passing Elberry Farm, a working farm and B&B and back to Broadsands car park where you began. After all of that healthy exercise you've definitely earnt an ice cream or hot chocolate.

DIRECTIONS

1 From Broadsands car park, head east with the sea on your left, past the new beach huts and turn right onto the coast path following the sign saying Torbay Circular Countryside Walk. Continue up the steps onto the grassy slope and follow the red path around Churston Point headland.
0.4 miles

2 Walk through the kissing gate, past the information sign and follow the path through the trees, bearing left to drop down onto the shingle beach, Elberry Cove. If you are swimming, do so from the nearside of the beach before continuing across the shingle towards the ruined bathing house.
0.1 miles

3 Walk through the entrance in the wall to the right of the bath house and up the steps, snaking through the trees. When you reach a large tree in the middle of the path (actually two trees, a sycamore and an ash), bear left to another gateway and a path down through Elberry and Marridge Woods, with the golf course on your right and the coast on your left.
0.9 miles

4 After about 20 minutes' walk, turn left at the next waymarker and then down the steps to Churston Cove. Enjoy another break here and perhaps a return swim over to Fishcombe Cove off to the right.
650 feet

5 Walk towards the near end of the beach (and not in the direction of Fishcombe) to enter The Grove. Walk up past the lime kilns and bear left at the next waymarker and then out of the woods through a stone gate and follow the sign for Churston Ferrers to the right, climbing over a stone stile. Walk along a section of the John Musgrave Heritage Trail to Churston Court Hotel.
1.1 miles

6 When you leave the hotel, walk past the church and then turn left past Churston Court Farm and walk straight ahead towards Broadsands and Links Close. Then turn right and immediately left and through a kissing gate onto the golf course.
0.3 miles

7 Follow the path over the course and through the yellow posts and then walk through bushes to a track. Turn right heading towards the sea and down the long track and through another kissing gate. Turn left at the fork, past the farm and back to Broadsands car park.
0.6 miles

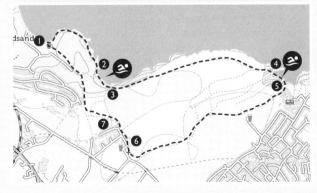

STAVERTON CIRCULAR

An old fashioned jape taking in steam trains, riverside rambles, adventurous swim spots, nature reserves, charming villages and some well-earned refreshment in a local pub.

T he short distance of this walk makes it reasonably accessible. Nevertheless you do get the impression that you are in the middle of nowhere, and a million miles away from home. A fun way to start this picturesque mini-adventure is by jumping on board the restored steam train at Littlehempston station in Totnes and chugging your way up to Staverton station. The track runs along the River Dart; make sure you sit on the left side of the train for the best views on the all-too-brief outbound journey. Alternatively you can travel from Buckfastleigh, and again the train follows the river, but from here you need to sit on the right to get the best views. Somewhat ironically the line must be the only one actually opened by Dr Richard Beeching, who as the head of British Rail had closed tracks and stations across the country. When the route was reopened in 1969, someone with a quirky sense of humour thought it might be amusing to invite Beeching to declare one open for a change.

Stepping off the train at Staverton you feel like you have walked into a gentle Sunday evening television drama, and indeed the station has been used as a location in everything from the *Hound of the Baskervilles* to *Five Go Mad in Dorset*. The charming country station looks the same as it would have done 100 years ago when it served the nearby village, as well as the 18th century corn mill and local farms, including those producing Devon cider. Real ale fans will also want to look out for the annual 'Rails and Ales' beer festival, held at the station every August bank holiday.

INFORMATION

PART OF THIS WALK IS CLOSED ON SUNDAYS

DISTANCE: 2 miles **TIME:** 1-2 hours
START POINT: Staverton Station (SX 783 637, TQ9 6FE). If you are planning to take the steam train (late March till end of October), park at one of the public car parks in Totnes and walk to Totnes Littlehempston Station, which is about 500 metres from the mainline station. Alternatively you can get the train from Buckfastleigh. The award-winning station has been built entirely from buildings and artefacts from GWR stations around the west. Or you can park at Staverton Station. Tickets cost 50p and are available from the station
END POINT: Staverton Station
PUBLIC TRANSPORT: Totnes has a mainline railway station and various bus links including the Gold bus service between Torquay, Totnes and Plymouth, the 88 from Newton Abbot and the X64 from Exeter
SWIMMING: Staverton Weir (SX 786 638), Still Pool (SX 791 636)
PLACES OF INTEREST: Staverton Bridge, Staverton Weir/Leat, Staverton Village, Staverton Nature Reserve
REFRESHMENTS: The Sea Trout Inn in Staverton is a long-established pub and hotel (01803 762274, TQ9 6PA) which prides itself on being dog-friendly. Just up the road from Staverton Station is the charming Staverton Bridge Nursery and Café, which bakes its own bread and grows its own salad (07866561088, TQ9 6NU)

Once you have fulfilled all your *Railway Children* fantasies, walk out of the station, cross the tracks and check out the pretty little bridge. Staverton or Stouretona means 'the village by the stony ford' and a crossing at this spot provided a route up to Dartington for centuries, before the present stone bridge with its seven stone arches was built around 1413. The photogenic structure even inspired a successful folk trio to call themselves Staverton Bridge in the 1970s. As tempting as it may look, you can't enter the water from here as the banks are private, including that of the mill, which has been converted into eight luxury dwellings. Indeed there is a very official looking sign warning canoeists not to egress here, so it's up to you if you decide to swim.

The walk takes you past the 18th century mill, which was built as a water-driven corn mill before being taken over by a group of gifted craftsmen in the 1930s, who had been restoring the Great Hall at Dartington. The beautiful building is both a Scheduled Ancient Monument and listed as Grade I. The walk takes you past lots of old railway stock, including one truck used to transport Teign Valley granite, and into the woods following the river. If you stop by the black and white bollard and then turn immediately back on yourself and through the two old gate posts, you can catch one of the few glimpses of the bridge that doesn't involve trespassing.

It's a delightful riverside walk through the trees, past several small beaches, until you reach the weir, originally built by fishermen. Some people like to swim here, while the area is also popular with canoeists who head down river through a fast chute in a broken section of the weir. The annual River Dart Raft Race also passes here.

You'll then arrive at Staverton Leat ❷ where the Totnes Renewable Energy Society are currently working on a plan to introduce a 100KW hydro power plant that can generate clean renewable electricity for Totnes. The site previously generated electricity for the Dartington estate in the 1920s. The plan is to generate electricity from an Archimedes turbine, as well as regenerating the leat and creating a new fish pass to help the up-and-down-stream migration of river life. The River Dart Country Park, further upstream, became the first place in the UK to use an Archimedes turbine for grid-connected power generation back in 2007.

Cross over the leat, over the top of the sluice gate, and enter what feels like a wooded island from an adventure story, with gnarly roots underfoot and the slow flow of the rust-coloured river glimpsed through gaps in the lush green jungle. It's a beautiful spot, completely unspoilt, and it's worth taking a moment to enjoy the river's lazy flow across the submerged pebbles, dappled by a canopy of overhanging trees. Carry on further over a bridge made from two old railway sleepers and onto a bench near a tree in the middle of the path. Here you can drop down onto the earthy beach and swim at the aptly named Still Pool ❸.

This popular swimming hole straight out of a Mark Twain story has been popular with generations of swimmers and it's easy to understand why. This naturally dammed playground has everything you need - a deep channel to swim through, a pebbly beach on the far shore to conquer and jumping rocks and a rope swing for the adventurous. The rugged old oak tree on the far shore has steps built into the trunk and has become a rite of passage for brave youths (and the odd wild swimmer) who jump

into the peaty waters below. Obviously always check the depth first, as rivers can change all of the time.

The walk continues across a private field (with access) and over the tracks at Nappers Halt and up towards the village ❹. You'll pass St Paul de Leon church, which recently celebrated the 700th anniversary of an edict by Bishop Walter de Stapleton to pull down the original Norman church and build a more capacious one. The vicar and parishioners were given 18 months to complete the enormous task. The new, bigger church wasn't always big enough though. Such was the size of the slate quarrying community living in the area in the 1850's, another church had to be built for their community at Landscove.

Continuing up the hill you'll pass The Court Room, which once housed an ecclesiastical court in centuries gone by and now serves as the village hall. It's then on to a refreshment stop at the dog-friendly Sea Trout Inn. Dating back to the 15th century, this popular inn also has exclusive rights to fishing on the nearby stretch of river, and is understandably popular for fishing breaks.

The walk continues down a footpath around the rear of the church and past charming cottages and artisan businesses, before heading back down towards the railway track and into a nature reserve ❺ owned and managed by Staverton Wildlife Regeneration Society. When the council was about to sell off this area of untouched woodland of considerable ecological importance in 2014, a group of parishioners formed a community society to raise funds to purchase the land themselves. A boardwalk takes you through the nature reserve before you head up some steps and walk past the pavilion and playing fields, and onto the lane. It's then just a short walk back to the station past charming B&Bs and an antiques shop.

will find the Sea Trout Inn on your left.
0.4 miles

❹ Once refreshed, leave the pub and walk back down the lane and turn right onto the footpath just before the church. Continue down the track and onto a lane turning left at Sweet William Cottage and into the woods.
0.4 miles

❶ Cross over the tracks and turn left onto the gravel track down the side of the old mill building. Continue along the riverside walk and pass the weir until you reach workings at the leat. Turn right to cross the sluice gates and into the woods.
0.4 miles

❷ The path winds its way through the woods with all tracks leading out again, but if in doubt take the left fork. Continue over a bridge made from two railway sleepers and on until you come to a bench near a tree in the middle of the path. Walk down the slope onto the 'beach' by the swimming spot, Still Pool.
0.3 miles

❸ Continue the walk by going back up the bank and turning right. Cross the private land (with access Monday to Saturdays only) and through the gate, turning left down the track. Cross over the railway at Nappers Halt and over the leat, before heading up the lane into the village. Pass the church and the village hall and you

❺ When you reach the railway tracks, don't cross them, but instead walk into the nature reserve through the wooden gate. Follow the wooden walkway through the reserve and then up some steps to emerge just below the tennis courts.
0.1 miles

❻ Walk along the bottom of the playing fields, past the playpark and then left onto the lane. Follow this back to the station where the walk began.
0.1 miles

TEIGNMOUTH TO DAWLISH RAILWAY WALK

A stunning walk taking in Brunel's world-famous coastal stretch of railway, as well as the famous red cliffs of South Devon.

O n this walk you can swim around and through two of Devon's more unusual and quirkily-named rock formations and sea stacks, as well as enjoy stunning views over to the Jurassic Coast.

The walk begins at Teignmouth Pier, which was built in 1865 and once provided a landing stage for pleasure steamers and boasted a pavilion complete with a ballroom. As well as offering traditional seaside entertainment including magic lantern shows, stuntmen would also entertain the crowds. The most famous was one-legged Peg Leg Pete, who would thrill onlookers by setting himself alight and diving from an impressive height into the sea below. The Grand Pier also provided a grandstand for crowds to watch water polo matches and indeed, members of the Teignmouth Team were Devon champions for many years. The structure once marked the segregation point for bathers with gentlemen's bathing machines to the west and ladies' to the east.

The pier may have survived the bombing raids of World War II (the town was bombed 21 times) but it almost didn't survive the storms of 2014. Powerful waves ripped through the wooden floors, causing hundreds of thousands of pounds worth of damage, closing the attraction for almost six months. As one of only two piers left on the south west coast (along with Paignton Pier) and one of only 50 original structures in England and Wales still standing, it is fortunate that the pier survived. The attraction is loved by many, including local band Muse, who used the iconic pier in the publicity for their homecoming Seaside Rendezvous gigs, which took place on the nearby Den - a big green space on the seafront - in 2009.

Perambulating along the seawall past the East Cliff Café and the yacht club, you'll be participating in an activity that has been

INFORMATION

DISTANCE: 3 miles (or 6 miles depending on whether returning by train)
TIME: 2-3 hours
MAP: OS Explorer, Teignmouth and Dawlish OL44
START POINT: Teignmouth Pier (SX 941 727, TQ14 8BB); parking on the seafront and in numerous car parks
END POINT: Teignmouth Pier
PUBLIC TRANSPORT: Teignmouth is served by train and buses including the Number 2 from Exeter and the 184 and 186 from Newton Abbot
SWIMMING: Holcombe Beach (the Parson and Clerk) (SX 957 746), Coryton Cove (SX 961 760)
PLACES OF INTEREST:
Teignmouth, Teignmouth Pier, The Riviera Line railway, the Parson and Clerk, Dawlish
REFRESHMENTS: The Eastcliff Café in Teignmouth is perfectly placed on the seafront (01626 777621, TQ14 8SH) with nice hot food including bacon baps, chips and teacakes. For a seafood extravaganza head to the Crab Shack (booking essential) (01626 777956, TQ14 8BY). In Dawlish, Gay's Creamery is an institution, serving pasties and ice creams (01626 863341, EX7 9PD).

popular since Victorian times. This coast-hugging stretch of railway line, one of the most picturesque in the world, was built to the designs of Isambard Kingdom Brunel as part of his Penzance-Paddington Line, and opened in 1846. What makes the ambitious route so stunning for passengers is also what can be its greatest threat, with the sea regularly battering this section of track. In 2014, the storms created a series of landslips which blocked the line. The seawall was so badly breached at Dawlish it left sections of railway track dangling in the air. The main rail link in and out of the south west was closed for two months. Repairs cost in excess of £35 million, and you'll be able to spot several suggestions of the Herculean effort of workers to get the line reopened in the red cliffs above you as you continue the walk.

The Teignmouth sign at Sprey Point is a good place to pause and take in the views back towards Teignmouth, the red cliffs of The Ness in Shaldon and beyond. The curious manmade headland halfway along the railway walk was built by Brunel in 1839, when he flattened a huge landslip and used it to land materials employed in the construction of the railway line. Between the wars, this spot with its amazing views became a popular location for strolling holidaymakers. There was a 'Halfway Café,' a tea garden and a games area where they could play bagatelle and table tennis. When the Second World War broke out, military defences were built here and the café closed, never to reopen.

Continuing on towards the tunnel, look out for an old lime kiln on the other side of the railway track, used in the construction of the line. You'll also see more groynes half buried in the sand. These are wooden structures built at right angles to the coast, to prevent the sand and pebbles being carried away by waves and tides. These make Teignmouth the

perfect place for swim training, with these wooden distance markers along the route.

Parson's Tunnel is the longest in a series of five impressive tunnels cut through the red cliffs here (Parson's Tunnel, Clerk's Tunnel, Phillot Tunnel, Coryton Tunnel and Kennaway Tunnel). You'll also be able to see the 'Parson' and 'Clerk' to the right of the tunnel – although this is the source of some disagreement. Locals think that the 'Parson' is the stack on the end of the cliff (which goes out of view closer to the tunnel), while the 'Clerk' is the stack just off the shore. The OS map begs to differ, calling the stack in the sea 'Shag Rock'. Who is right is anyone's guess. We've also heard it referred to as 'witches hat' and even 'Cock Rock'. It used to be much larger, but it lost its head in a storm in 2003.

As you'd expect there's a legend attached to the name of the rocks. When the Bishop of Exeter fell ill, an ambitious local priest had his eye on succeeding him following his demise. This parson and his clerk would often make the journey to Dawlish, where the Bishop was convalescing, to check on his

health. One night they made the journey during a terrible storm, and they found themselves lost on Haldon Moor. In his anger and frustration the priest shouted at his clerk that he would rather have the devil himself than him for a guide. At that very moment, a horseman appeared from nowhere and offered to be their escort. After a few miles they came across a dazzlingly lit mansion in Holcombe and the guide invited them in to sample his hospitality. While they were enjoying a sumptuous feast, news arrived that the bishop had died. Eager to secure his chance of promotion, the priest hurried the clerk and the guide to leave at once. However, when they jumped on the horses, the beasts refused to move. When use of his whip and spurs failed, the angry priest yelled "Devil take the brutes." At once the gleeful guide cried "Thank you sir" and shouted "gee up". The horses galloped over the cliff, carrying the parson and clerk on their backs. The devil then turned them to stone, forever pointing seaward as monuments to greed and ambition.

You can swim anywhere along the beach of course, but we like to get in right at the northern end, just by the Parson and Clerk, and the railway tunnel. Swimming through the enticing arch at the end of the protruding cliff is an amazing experience, best done on a flat sea, but we once had enormous fun in easterly winds, being bounced towards it and whooshing through. When it's calm, and the sea is clear, it can be truly serene, swimming underneath the beautiful red sandstone of the arch above, and going through to the secret beach that is only accessible to swimmers or boaters. You may well meet a kayaker or two.

After the swim, the steep walk up the evocatively titled Smugglers Lane should get you nicely warmed up, while imagining the clandestine activities that inspired the name. Illicit goods would be transported up this lane from Holcombe Beach to the village of Holcombe itself. According to local legend there is also a cave near the Parson and Clerk that leads to the garden of Sunnylands, a house which you'll pass as you walk along the main road at the top. Indeed when the railway tunnel was being built, workers apparently cut through a smugglers tunnel and blocked it off. A friend of ours, Gilly, who grew up in the area, shared these tantalising details:

"I've numerous, fond childhood memories of swimming at the Parson and Clerk, intermittently having to leg it up the stone steps to snatch train numbers on passing locomotives for my dad. There used to be a cave there - but we're going back 40-odd years since I last rounded the rocks, so rose-tinted memories might reveal only a semi-pathetic underhang instead. I first discovered it swimming round the corner from Coryton to Shell Cove. The tunnel was rough-cut cold, with slimy steps up inside, and a horizontal ledge or two with portholes looking out to sea. I never did dare venture to the top - I was stopped in my tracks by an ear-splitting roar as contrails in red, white and blue streamed past my port-hole vista. Yep, the Red Arrows were back in town for their annual aerobatic display!"

After a brief walk along the busy A379 you are soon on the South West Coast Path and walking a track sandwiched between two hedges that were laden with juicy blackberries when we researched the walk. Suddenly the hedge drops on your left to reveal the most extraordinary view down over Dawlish. The two rocks you can see below are Horse Rocks (the horses of the doomed Parson and Clerk), with Shell Cove just before them and our next swim stop at Coryton Cove just beyond that. On a clear day you can see a great deal of the Devon and Dorset Jurassic Coast World Heritage

Site, which stretches from Exmouth right around to Swanage. The path becomes really steep as it drops down towards the railway line (look out for the Smuggler's Inn on your left), before climbing back inland past some highly manicured lawns and back to the road.

After walking past some desirable properties on the Old Teignmouth Road, you'll enter Lea Mount Park, with more wonderful views down to Dawlish. Indeed this viewpoint appears in many early postcards of the seaside town. It's then down the cliff path to the beach for a well-deserved swim and refreshments. Coryton Cove used to be known as the gentleman's bathing place and was once the training ground of local Fred Holman, who won a gold medal in the 200-metre breaststroke at the 1908 London Olympics (four years after the stroke was first introduced). It's a lovely spot for a dip, with Horse Rocks off to the right (one does actually resemble a sea horse), and the gap at the Parson and Clerk viewable in the distance. It's also a great place to swim at sun or moonrise, as it faces east. We once had a wonderful moonlit swim here with a fire. Shell Cove is reachable by walking along the shore at very low tides, but be careful not to get cut off.

After your swim, stroll back past the beach huts and Old Maid Rock in the sea and round the corner past Cowhole Rock into Boat Cove. If there aren't waves crashing over, walk along the seawall known as the Kings Walk, which was built to celebrate the coronation of Edward VII. You'll then arrive at the three pedestrian archways under the railway track called the Colonnade Viaduct. The beach here was once known as the ladies bathing place, a safe distance from the men swimming over at Coryton Cove. You are now in the quaint seaside town of Dawlish, famous for

the black swans, which have inhabited the brook since at least the early 1900s.

Once you've enjoyed a delicious ice cream or mouth-watering pasty from Gay's Creamery, run as a family business since 1925, it's then over to the station for the return train journey along the stunning stretch of coast. Make sure you sit on the left hand side for the wonderful sea views that have enchanted passengers for the past 170 years. Don't forget to try and hold your breath through one of the tunnels - you get to make a wish if you manage it! Back in Teignmouth, it's well worth visiting the Teign Heritage Centre, which boasts a restored Victorian bathing machine, old pier slot machines, diving treasures and a fascinating look at the town's long and remarkable relationship with the sea.

DIRECTIONS

1 Walk north along the promenade from the pier with the sea on your right, and continue past Teignmouth Lido and the Teign Corinthian Yacht Club as the sea wall meets the railway. Continue past the enormous Teignmouth sign and on towards the railway tunnel.
1.4 miles

2 Drop down onto the beach at one of the last sets of steps for the first swim at Hole Head near Parson's Tunnel. After your swim, go back up the steps and under the archway onto Smugglers Lane. Walk up the steep hill to the main road. Carefully cross the busy road and turn right along the pavement. At the coast path sign, cross back over the road to turn right onto Windward Lane.
0.3 miles

3 After a short distance, turn left to join the South West Coast Path. Follow the path around the back of Hole Head and down the steep hill to join the railway again. Cross over the small bridge and then up the hill and out to the road again.
0.7 miles

4 Walk up the wooden steps onto the road. Turn right to follow the old Teignmouth Road and past some rather nice houses. Turn right into Lea Mount Gardens and follow the path left and down out of the gardens. Turn right at the fork and wind down the cliffs, turning right again to get to Coryton's Cove.
0.4 miles

5 After a swim, follow the path past the beach café and beach huts and

around the corner past Cowhole Rock and the breakwater to again join the railway line. Continue along the sea wall, left under the railway arch and then right along to the station. Cross over the tracks for the return train journey to Teignmouth. There are about four trains per hour at peak times and one each hour off-peak.
0.5 miles

To return to the pier in Teignmouth, walk straight out of the station, cross the road and walk down Station Road. Cross the road and onto the Triangle. Bear right and then cross the road at the new Pavilions art centre. Turn right and then left at the Tourist Information Centre to walk between the bowling club and the Den to reach the pier.
0.2 miles

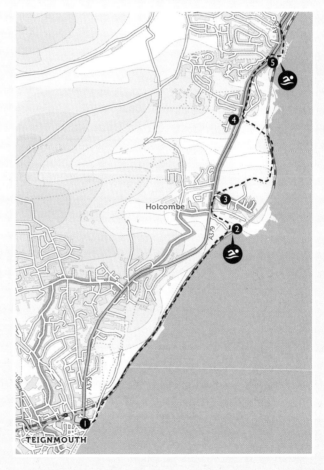

Moor Sands, p150

Health, Safety and
Responsibility. Like any
water-based activity, sea
swimming and coastal
exploration has risks
and can be dangerous
and these are described
more fully inside. Few of
the locations featured in
this book have lifeguards
and all are prone to tidal
immersion, currents and
sea-state changes. While
the author and publisher
have gone to great lengths
to ensure the accuracy of
the information herein they
will not be held legally or
financially responsible for
any accident, injury, loss or
inconvenience sustained as
a result of the information
or advice contained in this
book. Swimming, jumping,
diving, scrambling or any
other activities at any of
these locations is entirely at
your own risk.

Editor:
Hannah Hargrave
Cover illustration:
James Lewis
Design and layout:
Amy Bolt
Proofreading:
Michael Lee
Mapping powered by:

cycle.travel

Published by:
Wild Things Publishing Ltd
Bath, BA2 7WG,
United Kingdom
wildthingspublishing.com

WILD
THINGS
PUBLISHING

Acknowledgements

We'd like to thank the amazing community of wild swimmers in Devon, who have accompanied us on numerous walks, braved the extremes of Devon's weather, posed endlessly for photographs, and supplied vast quantities of cake, all with plenty of giggles along the way.

We'd particularly like to thank our talented photographer friends, including Dan Bolt, Sally Morgan, Ron Kahana, Allan Macfadyen, Shay Nichol, Chris Popham, Helen Sargent and Carole Whelan. Our partners Alex Murdin and Aaron Kitts, as well as doing a lot of the photography, have also provided invaluable support, everything from making packed lunches to sorting out IT issues!

We'd like to acknowledge our wonderful fellow swimmers and walkers for all their help and support: Tara Acton, Kay Arkinstall, Caroline Adams, Pauline Barker, Rosie Barnfield, Jane Brown, Lesley Chapman, Theresa Compton, Teri Cox, Helen Currell, Rachel Dawson, Stephanie D'Haussy, Lou Doret, Plum Duff, Anna Dunscombe, Hugo Durward, Kari Furre, Baa Goodwin, Judy Gordon Jones, Mark Green, Babette Grobler, Lauren Groch, Pippa and Simon Heywood, Ann Hogan, Ruth Jeffs, Lisa and Martin Kelman, Ben Kerr, Linda Knott, Mark Kilburn, Yaara Lahav, Karen and Jo Lubbe, Richard Lowerson, Katie Lusty, Allan Macfadyen, Kate Macfadyen, Nelia McHugh, Judy Marshall, Queenie Martin, Camilla McHugh, Sue Nightingale, Sara Palmer, David Pendleton, Clare Pettinger, Deb Phillips, Shirley Rees, Ellie Ricketts, Fleur Ricklin, Gilly Robinson, Catherine Rees Stephan, Alex Rees Stephan, Kate Rew, Carl Reynolds, Lynne Roper, Michele Sandhu, Johanna Sidey, Stephanie Simon, Catherine Townsend, Angie Watson, Kate Webb, Lynda Wilde, Alison Williams and Andrew Wilsdon.

Lastly we'd like to dedicate the book to Jonathan Joyce, an inspirational wild swimmer here in Devon, and inventor of the infamous 'Wildathon', in which he regularly cycled from his home in Ashburton to New Bridge on the River Dart, and then ran to Sharrah Pool where he swam. He was so much part of our community and died far too young.

Photo credits

All photos copyright Sophie Pierce and Matt Newbury, except: inside front cover, top Chris Popham, middle Dan Bolt, bottom Sally Morgan; inside back cover, top and middle Dan Bolt; P2 Chris Popham; P8 Aaron Kitts; P11 Dan Bolt; P12 top left Rachel Dawson, P12 top right Chris Popham, P12 bottom and P13 Dan Bolt; P14 left Miriam Aston-Hetherington, top right Aaron Kitts, bottom right Sally Morgan; P15, 16, Aaron Kitts; P18 Dan Bolt; P19 Top Aaron Kitts; P20, P21 right Aaron Kitts; P22 Dan Bolt; P23 Allan Macfadyen; P24 Dan Bolt; P35 bottom Lynne Roper; P42 top Ron Kahana; P44, P46, P48, P49 Aaron Kitts; P50 Alex Murdin; P53 bottom Rachel Dawson; P54 top Alex Murdin; P56 Dan Bolt; P66 Lynne Roper; P72 Alex Murdin; P74 Dan Bolt; P77 bottom Dan Bolt; P79 bottom Dan Bolt; P80 Allan Macfadyen; P82 top and P83 top Alex Murdin; P84 Chris Popham; P90, 92 Dan Bolt; P96 Top and P99 Alex Murdin; P100, 102, 103 Dan Bolt; P104 Daniel Start, P107 Dan Bolt; P114 Aaron Kitts; P116, 118, 120 Shay Nichol; P124, 125, 126 Sally Morgan; P128, 130 Carole Whelan; P139 Helen Sargent; P140, 143 146 Aaron Kitts; P154, 155 top right Sally Morgan; P156 Aaron Kitts; P158 Sally Morgan; P160 Aaron Kitts; P163 top, P164, P165 Aaron Kitts; P166, 168, 169, 171 Sally Morgan; P 172, 174, Aaron Kitts; P176 Richard Lowerson; P177, 178, 180, Aaron Kitts; P183 Lucian Murdin; P184, 186, 187, 188, 189, Aaron Kitts; P192 top Stephanie Simon; P 195, 196 Chris Popham, P201 top Martin Kelman, P206 Chris Popham, P 208 Babette Grobler.